The Land Unknown

KATHLEEN RAINE

The Land Unknown

Thel enter'd in & saw the secrets of the land unknown.
She saw the couches of the dead, & where the fibrous roots
Of every heart on earth infixes deep its restless twists.

THE BOOK OF THEL

If you would cleanse your mind of old delusions
From your many sins you would be freed.

MOTOME-ZUKA

GEORGE
BRAZILLER

NEW YORK

Published in the United States in 1975 by George Braziller, Inc.
Copyright © 1975 by Kathleen Raine
Originally published in England by Hamish Hamilton Ltd.

International Standard Book Number: 0–8076–0800–9
Library of Congress Catalog Card Number: 75–10995
Printed in the United States of America
First Printing

CONTENTS

INTRODUCTION

SOME TWELVE years ago I had reached a moment that
comes perhaps to all, when I found myself moved by
a compelling impulse to take stock of my life; to try to
understand my own life not so much because it had been
mine, but because our own lives are the only ones of which
each of us has personal and immediate experience. A life,
as such, is something so mysterious that to find its meaning
seems all-important. And if there is no meaning, has not
meaning to be invented? Created? Is that not what we are
all incessantly engaged in? We can report our findings to
others, but we can examine only ourselves. And we seem to
learn so much, and with such pain (given and received) that
we feel it matters, in some ultimate sense, to ourselves, to
one another, but also to some order of things outside our
knowledge. My friend Gay Taylor used to say that we are
food for higher spiritual heirarchies, a harvest for the angels;
but the corn too has its place in the order of things.

However, the point for me was the compulsion, at that
time, to examine my life as truthfully as I could (and no-one
can be more truthful than self-knowledge permits) and to
try to see, above all, where and why I had gone so often and
so obviously (in retrospect obviously) wrong.

The present volume is the second part of what I then
wrote. There is a third part—to me the most significant of
all, though, again, a record of disastrous mistakes—but
whether I shall publish that third section I do not know.
Now for many years I have lived a life both interesting and
agreeable but which seems to lie beyond the limits of
'autobiography' altogether. I do not know whether this is

a good thing or a bad thing. I have many interests, but these no longer include myself or anything that may befall me. Is this merely the normal condition of old age?

For personal reasons it would not have been possible to publish my record at the time I wrote it; and the publication of the present volume might have given pain to some I loved in 1972, when I did publish memories of childhood, under the title *Farewell Happy Fields*. Since I assumed, in the writing of what follows, that readers would have read the record as a whole, it is necessary here to give a short outline of what the earlier book contains.

I think my early childhood must have been an exceptionally happy one, though I hope many others remember, as I do, some Paradise. My own was simple enough—a bleak hamlet in Northumberland, where during the first world-war I was sent by my parents to live with an aunt who was the village schoolmistress. I suppose I was sent because food-shortages, 'flu, and the air-raids made life in the east-London surburb where I was born, difficult, even precarious. Enemy aeroplanes returning from raiding London often dropped their bombs as they went, and there was, besides, an aerodrome near us. All my mother's relations lived on one or the other side of the Border, and to my Scotch mother—and to myself—that country always remained 'home'. I attended Aunty Peggy's school, and was happy. Against those years I have measured all subsequent experience.

As for the suburb I hated it always; perhaps I reflected my mother's sense of exile and frustration, fortified by my own experience of her beloved North. My father was the English-master at the County High School, Ilford, and in his work as teacher and House-master, as a Wesleyan Methodist 'local preacher', and as a worker for pacifism and the League of Nations Union, he found fulfilment, loved and respected by many who remember him to this day. To him—and to the excellent teaching in the girls' department of the C.H.S.I.—I owe the foundations of an education few schools for the lower middle-class provide nowadays; but the imagaination of the poet has always remained a dweller on the Border hills.

While I was still very young, too young, another rebel against Ilford's values, a former pupil of my father's, and assistant organist at his Chapel fell in love with me. But if my paradisal dreams were of Northern wilds, his were nourished by Dowson and Hopkins and Flecker, Chopin and Debussy. My father's intervention in this early dream brought to an end the years of happiness, and I went up to Cambridge already filled with the sense of guilt, heartbreak, and potential rebellion.

My situation was further complicated by the discovery that a friend of my father's, a distinguished French schoolmaster and educationalist to whom I had looked as mentor and guide, had also fallen in love with me.

In these circumstances anyone but myself must have foreseen trouble ahead for myself and others.

CHAPTER ONE

Fool's Paradise

I CHOSE science at that moment when schoolchildren reach the parting of the ways; in part because I found the matter of science enthralling, in part because I felt no need to be 'taught' literature. One had only to read the books, after all; to be taught 'about' literature, which is itself the teaching, seemed to me a waste of time which could be better spent in learning what is not to be learned from books. I also chose science because our teacher of botany at that time was one of those rare people whose subject is a passion. She was herself still, at heart, a student (I believe she did, later, return to research), and communicated her enthusiasm to my two companions and myself in the science 'advanced course'. We spent long enchanted hours in the little botany laboratory, learning to cut and stain specimens for the microscope, to make detailed drawings of the marvellous structured beauty of plant-tissues; a world where form and meaning were one and indivisible. My father was satisfied because I had made a decision to work for a scholarship to Cambridge: the first step to a career. I was satisfied because in exploring the inexhaustible and lucid beauty of form and metamorphosis in nature I felt that I was approaching some secret source, or source of some secret. I was in love with the beauty of 'nature' but whether as a poet loves nature or as a scientist was not clear; or rather there seemed no difference, what I loved I loved. The two incompatible plans for my future for the time being coincided, my secret poetic vocation and my immediate delight in biology. When the ways would part I did not know. I worked hard; and with a small College

11

exhibition and a County Major scholarship I was admitted to Girton. My father was satisfied, my school was proud of me. That was to be the last moment, after childhood, when I was not at odds with the world.

At that time, too, my relationship with my father was, for the last time, unimpaired by guilt and remorse. If we were ever to meet in some other world I believe he would remind me of those mornings when, for an hour each day before breakfast, he taught me the rudiments of Latin grammar, and read with me, to our mutual delight, two books of Virgil and Horace's *Odes*, books III and IV. In those days it was necessary for every undergraduate at Cambridge to have passed 'Little Go' in Latin. As I had no Latin, my father taught me all I ever learned in the two or three months between my examination for Girton and the date of the Cambridge Previous Examination. He himself loved Latin only a little less than he loved Anglo-Saxon; loved grammar and the structure of language for its own sake; and he communicated to me some of that love. I remember some of those Odes by heart to this day. I knew my father, at that time, at his best; for with how few could he share that love of the ancient speech, the ancient learning, his own participation too seldom activated by the circumstances of his life. We seemed to walk together in an ancient civilized world.

When I passed that simple test I truly pleased him. All that turbid turmoil of religion and first love that had so embittered our relationship was forgotten as he taught me the Greek lyric metres, as Horace had used them; and scanned with me those famous hexameters of Dante's master. How often since, from the turmoil of emotion, I have sought and found sanctuary in the calm regions of the mind; and for this I have my father to thank. If he made that escape necessary he did, also, make it possible.

So little did I know of the world, so boundless were my dreams of what the realms of civilization had to offer, that I never doubted when, for the first time, I breathed the characteristic country-house scent of beeswax, lavender and chrysanthemums in the corridors of Girton that before me lay a future of unbroken happiness and freedom, leading to the realization of every hope. I was for the first time enjoying a little success, and standing in good credit with my elders, and with myself. Cambridge, because it was not Ilford, seemed to me paradise. I would henceforth spend my time among people of culture, in whose life of the mind, delightfully occupied with knowledge for its own sake, I would participate. These cultured companions would be mine; they would share my values and among them I would no longer be alone. Poets too I might meet—had not Milton and Gray and Wordsworth and Coleridge and many more gone up, as I was going now, as students to Cambridge? I had achieved what Jude the Obscure and Sue Bridehead had perished for the want of; I had escaped from the underworld.

With the same ease as that with which as a child I had entered the palaces and sat upon the golden thrones of some fairy-tale in the person of the Princess, and into a like unreality, I now stepped into the enchantment of Girton. From the lowest table in Hall I looked up at those great and learned ladies who, in lustrous Italian silks and velvets, with Victorian smooth-parted hair, seemed, at High Table, high indeed; as some of them really were. Tall, beautiful Miss Allen, then bursar of the College, had once, as a suffragette, been chained, so it was said, to the railings of Hyde Park. Now, as under the rule of some royal Abbess, she and her sister dons enjoyed the fruits of their triumph, that beautiful and happy College. There is a world of difference between the admitting of the sons or daughters of the obscure into court or monastery or college to live among an aristocracy (of learning, of religion, or of some other kind) and to learn its ways, and the looting of palace or abbey or college by the crowd, whose total possession can but be a total dispossession. For the looted palace is no longer a palace at all, nor colleges places of that learning which revolution sweeps away. There is a great difference between the situation of the poor students of my generation, who really were admitted—

albeit to an extent more limited than we ourselves realized—into a higher social class, with a tradition and a culture different from, and superior to, our own, and the present situation of such students (even in Oxford and Cambridge) who, being now in the majority, create their own standards. In my student days we were the exceptions; and we were able to learn, to assimilate something from those—still in the majority—who inherited the old culture of England's educated classes. Young barbarians of talent such as myself could still, at that time, to some extent become assimilated into social structures which, by our very number, we were, within a generation, to destroy. It was not our intention to kill the thing we loved, but by force of number we have done so. Unwittingly, unwillingly, we were the first wave of the deluge.

That is of course a sweeping overstatement; no revolution is ever wholly successful in destroying the older culture, and much, thank God, survives, and much is transmitted still to generations of students in Universities whose brick is even newer and redder than that of Girton. But so much at least is true—that in those days revolution was the last thing we wished for. We respected the inherited standards of excellence with no thought of changing them. The dons of Girton believed no less than did the Masters and Fellows of other colleges in the culture they had fought for women's right to share. We as students believed no less in the value of what they had won for us; perhaps even more, the known being limited, the unknown, boundless. Athens, Rome, Florence, all the glory of learning once contained in the word 'Renaissance', cast their magic on my expectation of what Cambridge would be. All knowledge, I thought, was there; as if knowledge and learning existed in a world of its own, in books and libraries. I did not understand that there is no such immortal being as 'civilization', only civilized people; and the continuance of a culture depends upon those who receive its inheritance.

At Girton, then, I first began to study my part, leaving behind the poor natural maiden who would have been content to be Roland's Lyric Love. Girton was itself the first building in which, by its proportions, its architecture (it was then the fashion to decry Victorian Gothic, but Girton, as an example of that style, is not without distinction) imposed certain intangible values and standards. On those lawns, in those cool corridors, I found myself conforming my behaviour to the architecture and the spacious scale of buildings and garden; walking with a prouder poise, with a sense of being visible to others of my own kind.

On the pavements of Ilford I had shrunk into myself in shame, physically present there against my will, elsewhere in spirit. Is not the chief pleasure we experience from architecture (and perhaps from all other arts, though in less obvious ways) the change it imposes upon ourselves? The justification of the cost and labour of Gothic cathedrals and Renaissance palazzos is the greatness they confer upon, and demand of, those who come and go in them, inducing in us civilized modes of being and behaviour. The mean streets of the Ilfords of the world impose meanness of thought, make impossible, or all but impossible, certain kinds of feeling, certain modes of consciousness; or drive these into bookish dreams. Conversely, in order to escape the silent demands of dignified and beautiful proportions, barbarians must desecrate and violate, smash the stained glass and deface the statues and paint defiant slogans on walls that tell us too clearly, in their beauty and harmony of proportion, that we might be better than we are.

We lived in an environment still beautiful, still within the fast-vanishing culture that had raised these buildings, the last inheritors of certain moods and modes of consciousness communicated by the very architecture of the colleges and the sound of the English language as spoken by a cultured class. So all Romans continue, in a certain sense, contemporaries of Michelangelo and Bramante because their works have formed an environment which continues to exist. We do not inhabit only the present; yet the forms of the past may conceal from us destructive forces which their own different affirmations have become powerless to negate

15

Dazzled by the façade of Cambridge I did not perceive that it was the architecture of the Cavendish, not of King's or Trinity Great Court, or even of neo-Gothic Girton, that corresponded to the new standards of quantitative, scientific 'truth', to the Cambridge of the present. I did not realize that the new thought which inhabited the Gibbs Building, the Senate House, the Gothic and Renaissance courts and libraries, the Victorian avenues of elm and lime, was no longer that which had built them and which their forms continued to express and communicate. I sang with the Madrigal Society Vivaldi and Palestrina, with the University Musical Society Vaughan Williams and Bach, without realizing that the opinions I was at the same time imbibing were destructive to the very foundations upon which such beauty rests; for the English language spoken so beautifully by young men from the great Public Schools, acting Shakespeare's plays on summer evenings in College gardens by the Cam, seemed still the living speech of a living culture.

In the mid-nineteen-twenties revoltion was not yet in the air. We did not know, young fresh folk as we were, that we were living in the last years of that European civilization of whose architecture, whose literature, whose thoughts we were the heirs. There was no mention of a 'third world' in those days; and even socialism (like my father's), was liberal; asking not for the destruction of a civilization, but that more people should participate in it. That was what I, and I suppose most of my fellow-students, hoped for, and believed would come about through the spread of education. I had not read Dante then, but such idealists as my father did not need Dante to spell out for them the truth that, whereas material goods are diminished by sharing, the spiritual treasuries of knowledge and of beauty, of poetry, music and the rest, by being shared are not diminished but increased. So I then believed, and so I do now. Marxism and other materialist ideologies have coloured current attitudes (I write now in 1974) towards the spiritual heritage of civilization with the same envy (or justifiable sense of injustice) that prevails in the politics of material wealth. The posses-

16

sion of knowledge, of culture, is now under attack as 'privilege', regardless of the fact that it is a privilege none need possess to the exclusion of others. I remember how shocked I was (and this was a theme much discussed among my friends) by Huxley's suggestion, in *Brave New World*, that batches of unintelligent people should be bred, in his Utopia, to perform the duller tasks. Rather, we then thought, technology should remove such tasks altogether, enabling all to live cultured lives. But the irrational tide of revolution is not to be turned; and western civilization— the civilization of the Cambridge I knew—is doomed and already largely gone; with all that subtle beauty and know-ledge, the mental spaciousness and freedom, the breadth of humanity, the insights, the never-to-be repeated quality of life created and enjoyed by the race C. S. Lewis (one of its last representatives, as he told us) called 'old western man'. Revolution follows its own laws; and the new age belongs to races and classes who, because they had no part in Old Western culture, will not inherit but supplant; supplant not because the old culture was good or bad but because it was never theirs.

Meanwhile we children of the *entre-deux-guerres* enjoyed our world without any sense of guilt or doom. The acquiring of its knowledge, the participation in its culture, seemed un-questionably good; and those standards of excellence in-herent in every art or science the self-evident standards set for all those who studied or practised them. No one had as yet called in question, or sought to destroy, or to replace, the values of Virgil, Dante, Spenser and Shakespeare and all that unity of culture that lies between Homer and T. S. Eliot. These, for us, were the norm, the measure and scope of our humanity as such. Eliot indeed was our master, in the late 1920s, and it was he who taught us, precisely, to value, to preserve, to transmit, enriched (if we could) but in no circumstances diminished, our inheritance. He had written: 'Someone said, "The dead writers are remote from us because we *know* so much more than they did." Precisely, and they are that which we know.' He wrote, too, of a new Dark

17

Age approaching; but that thought only made our present seem more joyously bright. Our Age was not dark.

Certainly I took too much for granted, even by the standards of those days. I felt no gratitude, so far as I remember, only delicious pride. I believed I had been admitted to Girton because of my deserts. During our first week the Mistress (a figure much like Queen Victoria in my eyes, and indeed her dumpy figure was of the same unqueenly cast) had told the 'freshers' assembled in the Stanley Library of the great privilege which was ours, of the many called and the few chosen. We were an elect, and of this we were well aware. Every woman admitted to the relatively few available places at the two women's colleges must have reached what was, in the men's colleges, scholarship standard. So it was said and so we willingly believed. It was for us, by our work, to justify our election. Perhaps it was this belief, held rightly or wrongly in the two women's colleges (Girton was, after all, a first triumph of the Victorian feminist movement) which has made my own attitude to men in general one of faint intellectual condescension; an attitude of which I only become aware as I remember that all Girtonians believed themselves the mental equals of the best of the men. So do Etonians and Wykehamists instinctively behave towards the rest of the world. They (like Girtonians) are always prepared to grant that Etonians and Wykehamists are in no way necessarily superior to others; but the unconscious attitude remains, and is based, after all, not on personal vanity but on a justified belief in the excellence of those schools. We who in 1926 went up to our Cambridge colleges believed in the excellence both of the education and the culture transmitted by our University; we did not doubt the social value of an educated élite; nor, for that matter, of a hereditary élite by whose presence among us were transmitted those imponderable qualities of English culture book-learning alone cannot give.

Mine was the Girton of Rosamond Lehmann's novel *Dusty Answer*; published the year I went up. I remember the Mistress asking a group of us (invited, as was the custom, in small batches to take coffee in that elegant sanctum, 'the Mistress's room') whether we thought *Dusty Answer* gave a true picture of life in College. I tactlessly said I thought it did; not an answer to meet with official approval. The Mistress could hardly have seen with Rosamond Lehmann's eyes (or with ours) the 'godlike young men' who in those days, when examination requirements were less stringent, adorned the Backs, the river, and the courts of Magdalene, Trinity and King's. The phrase 'godlike young men' was current in Girton; and only half in irony, after all. Neither in Florence nor in Athens, nor in Murasaki's Kyoto, could our young aristocracy have been surpassed in that well-bred grace of good looks enhanced by good manners, and by the possessors' own carefree assurance of their own god-likeness. We loved our lords. Innocent of politics, no sense of guilt clouded our enjoyment; a moment of civilized youth, whose joyous freedom will perhaps never come again.

Now all these values are called in question; and asking myself in all truth what I have to say to the egalitarians, I offer an image. Suppose human society to be a pyramid whose base is everyman's due, and whose apex the highest attainable human excellence. Somewhere between base and apex we each must find our place; but never must the standards of excellence be lost or corrupted, for to realize the highest excellence is perhaps the task of our race in the economy of the universe. Those who give expression, whether in knowledge or in moral or aesthetic beauty, to the highest things, are giving to the world patterns of a perfection to which all must strive, which is latent in all. Through the creations of the few we all live, somewhat, in Genji's court, in Plato's Academy, in Mme. Verdurin's salon. If not to enrich, to cultivate, to extend the scope of know-ledge, to refine the perceptions of consciousness; ultimately to attain what in the Far East is called 'enlightenment'—spiritual knowledge—what is the task of life, what its meaning?

I belong to the generation of C. S. Lewis, who wrote

19

'Human life means to me the life of beings for whom the leisured activities of thought, art, literature, conversation are the end, and the preservation of life merely the means.' I also believe that it is better to admire than to envy; to give honour where honour is due; or even to give honour where no honour is due, since admiration creates the fragile world of beauty, creates our Helens and our Hamlets; perhaps, even (as in India the Guru is honoured for the divine in him, not denigrated for his feet of clay) also our saints and our sages; while envy can only destroy that intangible lost domain of imagined perfection. And what we imagine, we create. It is our own humanity that grows by what we honour, it is the royal image in ourselves that our iconoclasms destroy. Strange (so it seems to me, writing in 1974 of my youth nearly fifty years ago) that the very premises of civilization should stand in need of defence.

Psyche's house did not seem to her more wonderful than did Girton to me, with its lawns and rare Victorian flowers and trees and drifts of Tennysonian violets, its still libraries, where light, as in some pre-Raphaelite painting or romance, filtered through cedar-boughs and amethyst-tinted panes upon Victorian busts of the learned and the great, and Flaxman's little marble winged figure of Psyche herself. Years later I stayed with my friend Winifred Nicholson at Boothby, the last home of that great feminist the Countess of Carlisle, daughter of Lady Stanley, one of the founders of the College; and I recognized there the same indefinable atmosphere of the life of great Victorian ladies of 'plain living and high thinking' that in my student days I had breathed at Girton. The scent of beeswax and lavender, the immaculate housekeeping, the daily rhythm that gives a sense of timeless present; as if this good way were the only possible way of life from time immemorial. Because of the dreams of Lady Stanley and her friends, that rich heritage of English culture at its finest was thrown open to such unmade creatures as myself, in the hope and belief that we in our turn would carry and transmit that tradition. I hope and believe that even now the transmission continues.

So in my first term, as I sped down Castle Hill on my bicycle, and along Trinity Street and King's Parade on my way to the science buildings of Downing Street, I used to declaim aloud,

> Is it not passing brave to be a king
> And ride in triumph through Persepolis?

The sense of glory was a radiance that cast no shadow. All things were possible, I was free, I was in my own world at last.

My life in College seemed at first like a dream, a painted scene, as if life here were made of a different stuff from any reality I had hitherto known; as in a sense it was, though not in the way I thought. The difference lay in no magic light cast on the scene, but in a kind of consciousness; in what, for educated people, constitutes reality; to what themes, experiences, happenings, the attention of the mind is directed; what is noted, what disregarded. I did not see what were the demands made upon those who, like myself, wished to participate. I thought, paddler that I was, that by merely being among swans I had become one.

It was during the summer term that Virginia Woolf visited Girton—the first famous person with whom I had ever been in the same room. She came—it is all history now—at the invitation of the Girton Literary Society, to give her paper, *A Room of One's Own*. The meeting took place in Girton's reception-room, with its mural panels, the work of a benefactor of the College who, having lived before the benefits of higher education, had devoted those long, idle Victorian hours (what happened to all that abundance of time after the turn of the century?) to embroidering in wool on ivory satin rather heavy foliage and flowers and birds and squirrels for the pleasure of those ladies who were to be educated away from the immemorial and symbolic occupations of Helen, Penelope, Persephone, and Blake's Daughters of Albion. The portrait of Lady Carew herself, in voluminous blue silk, hung over the chimney, reminding us that the eye of the Liberal aristocracy was upon all our comings and

21

goings. The grand piano, draped with a piece of oriental embroidery, was pushed to one side. Outside those tinted neo-Gothic windows cedar and tulip tree spread their branches over the sweep of the lawns upon whose green cedar-shaded carpet I was now no trespasser, but one of the happy and thrice-happy permitted to walk.

In the fairyland of the Girton reception-room, then, members of the Literary Society were gathered for coffee, after Hall; young Eton-cropped hair gleaming, Chinese shawls spread like the plumage of butterflies. (I vainly longed for one of those shawls, fringed with silk and embroidered with silken flowers and birds, fashionable at that time.) With Virginia Woolf had come her friend Victoria Sackville-West: the two most beautiful women I had ever seen. I saw their beauty and their fame entirely removed from the context of what is usually called 'real' life, as if they had descended like goddesses from Olympus, to reascend when at the end of the evening they vanished from our sight. The divine *mana* may belong to certain beings merely by virtue of what they are; but *mana* belongs also to certain offices, royal or priestly; and masters in some art were, in those days, invested with the dignity of their profession. A 'great writer' had about him or about her an inherited glory shed from the greatness of writers of the past; and about Virginia Woolf this glory hovered. Every sacred office can be discredited, and in the present world, in England, the profession of the writer has been brought into disrepute by the same looting of sanctuaries as has taken place in other spheres of life.

I had not read any of Virginia Woolf's novels at the time; a few months before I had not even heard of her. Now from her famous paper I learned for the first time, and with surprise, that the problems of 'a woman writer' were supposed to be different from the problems of a man who writes; that the problem is not one of writing but of living in such a way as to be able to write. *A Room of One's Own* made claims on life far beyond mine: a room and a small unearned income were, to me, luxuries unimaginable. To elude the

22

vigilance of my parents, and to write poems on the marble-topped table of a Lyons' or an ABC tea-shop was all I had at home, or for long after, hoped for. At Girton I had a room of my own; but while feeling it my due, I did not, at the same time, expect it to last, any more than a dream lasts; and yet, within that dream, we accept all that comes as a matter of course.

The pioneers to whom Girton owed its foundation had fought for the freedom I there enjoyed. Even so, I cannot truthfully say that I have ever found that my problems as a writer have been made greater or less by being a woman. The only problem—to write well and to write truly—is the same for either sex. As for time to write, there is always time. Volumes might have been written in the time Lady Carew spent on all that wool embroidery upon satin. But perhaps the embroidery was a wiser choice, after all.

But how I loved my College room of my own—two rooms, in fact, a small bedroom and a little sitting-room in 'Top Old'. In the morning, our 'gyp' brought to each of us a can of hot water, set it in our wash-basin, and covered it with a towel. And we each had a coal-fire (also laid for us daily) and a graceful oval copper kettle, polished on top (the kettles of the dons were polished all over). Each of us had our own desk, writing-chair, arm-chair, and bookshelves, with curtains and covers of fresh clean linen; in many of the rooms still of the original William Morris designs, very old-fashioned it was fashionable to think, in those days when Heal's furniture and the rectilinear style were new. We added, of course, our own touches. We had our toasting-forks, from which we dropped our Matthews' crumpets into the fire; I bought some hand-woven blue material, and put up two rhyme-sheets, one, of William Allingham's 'Four ducks in a pond', the other Blake's 'Never seek to tell thy love'. Some of us had Byron's 'We'll go no more a-roving/ So late into the night'. The choice of rhyme-sheets was restricted.

We considered ourselves emancipated, for the chaperon rules had recently been relaxed; and now two or more students might entertain young men in their rooms, to tea, if permission was obtained in writing, from the Mistress, the names and colleges of all students present being given. We dropped our neatly folded notes into the Mistress's letter box the previous day, and as a matter of course received our permission. This was seen as a great advance. A friend some ten years my senior remembers permission being refused to a friend who had been invited to accompany her father and herself on the river; the friend was a daughter of one of her father's fellow Ministers in Asquith's Cabinet. Yet another relaxation, new in my year, allowed students to carry their own parcels from Cambridge; mostly, even so, we had our orders from Matthews' cake-shop, or Heffers' book-shop, delivered at the College.

No more than we felt guilt as a privileged élite (words with no anti-social connotations in those days) did we feel ourselves 'victimized' by the strict rules under which we lived and worked. If a few habitually, and most of us once or twice, broke the rule of being in College by 10 p.m., and climbed in through a window into a ground-floor room, that was at our own risk, and for the sake of the adventure. We were only too glad to live in that College, the very realization of Tennyson's *The Princess*; to visit one another's rooms, like schoolgirls, for sophisticated coffee, or homely 'jug' (cocoa at 9 p.m.). Most were still virgins at the end of our three years; nor was it the virgins among us who were neurotic, restless, dissatisfied and liable to breakdowns, but the 'emancipated' minority who were not. As I remember it seems to me that living as a student in Girton was one of the few perfectly happy times of my life; but happy as a dream is happy, as something that had befallen me; not, as my years at Bavington, a time when the world, its hills and skies, its simple tasks and simple people were like a part of myself.

But there was another side to my entry into this world, where most of the students, the women no less than the men, were members of the upper or upper-middle classes. Most had been to public schools or to some of the more famous grammar schools. People like myself were still in a minority, I did not recognize in myself a social phenomenon, the first wave of the 'filthy modern tide'; on the contrary, I thought I had myself escaped drowning and crossed a social barrier because I had passed an examination. The fact that I was in those days considered by some people (including myself) to be beautiful, confused the issue still further for me: I expected to be accepted. I thought myself talented and beautiful; had not M. d'H seen in me the swan I felt myself to be? But I soon discovered that in Girton I was no swan. Those beatuiful well-groomed young women from Cheltenham and St. Leonard's Ladies' Colleges who all seemed to have come up already knowing one another, or with friends in common, with brothers and cousins in the men's colleges, were of another race. They were merely continuing to live within a world which was already theirs; no metamorphosis was demanded of them. From afar I admired these proud creatures who came and went with ease and assurance. I would gladly have resembled them, but I did not; they knew, and I knew.

One, I remember, whose dignified beauty and whose clothes (so simple that I in my naïvety could not imagine why my own home-made garments looked so different) I had admired afar off, invited me, with other science students in our first term, to tea; she was herself a medical student. She said, assuming agreement from us all, that she thought it a pity that girls from secondary schools should be admitted to Girton. I blushed so deeply that she became as embarrassed as myself, and apologized; but it had been said. After that I avoided her, and the other bright ones. My friends were therefore, of necessity, the outsiders. I was on surer ground with my fellow-scientists, for in the labs I was accorded my due, no more, no less; but what I really wanted was to meet the other cygnets of the species of which I believed myself an 'ugly duckling'—the writers.

Following a College tradition, first-year students formed themselves into 'families'—small groups of four or five, who were thereafter considered to be the little cell in the College organism to which you belonged during the remainder of your three years. So far as I know no one ever changed her family; the feeling of the College was against this; and so to an arbitrary and premature choice we were thereafter committed. Yet it was, in many ways, a happy arrangement; no one was, at all events, lonely or left out. The most interesting member of my 'family' was the senior scholar of my year, a Jewish moral scientist, the first Marxist I had met. She, as a member of a persecuted race, I an 'outsider' by reason of class, were thrown together. She introduced me to the avant-gardism of the time, to the books of Aldous Huxley, Virginia Woolf, E. M. Forster, Lytton Strachey and the rest of the Bloomsbury school; and to Roger Fry's and Clive Bell's books on painting. I had hitherto supposed that the object of painting was to produce likenesses of beautiful persons and of the beauties of nature; but now I read with wonder of 'significant form'. I remember especially those Giottos illustrating the doubtful theory, and the overwhelming impression they made on me. My friend had a reproduction of the *Pietà* in her study, and with what a sense of liberation I learned to dissociate the aesthetic from the religious content of Giotto's eloquent linear figures. If I have come full circle to the opposite view, that meaning and form are indivisible, 'significant form' was, none the less, at that time a most liberating new way of seeing.

I soon discovered, by the scorn of my new friends, that *The Spirit of Man*, Keats and Shelley, Yeats and the other Irish poets, Walter de la Mare, and Thomas Hardy, my old passions, were not the thing at all; nor my old love Roland's *The Hound of Heaven* and Swinburne and Dowson and Flecker. D. H. Lawrence, I to my astonishment discovered, was in the new pantheon. This greatly surprised me, for in Brittany M. d'H had lent me *The Captain's Doll*, which I had found both ridiculous and distasteful. I now read *Sons and Lovers* and *The White Peacock*, and found them much inferior to *Jude the Obscure* or *The Return of the Native*. When I later read other of his novels. *Aaron's Rod* and *Women in Love* and the rest, I found Lawrence's ill-mannered and sex-obsessed people coarse and low-class; I could identify myself with Tess or Sue Bride-head, but not with these fleshy Gudruns and gauche Miriams. Why, besides, should I be asked to read books about the very underworld I was struggling to get away from? It was as if the filthy modern tide were wetting my heels as I scrambled to safety. It is true that I had not altogether under-stood either Hardy or Lawrence; I now realize that, in his essays above all, Lawrence saw and deplored the social dis-placement he himself at once represented and described, with no less grief than Hardy. Conversely, Hardy, like Lawrence, had foreseen the vanishing of the traditional rural world—the world of my own roots, and my earliest loyalty —and of its people. I now see that Jude and Sue were Lawrence's people, already foreseen, uprooted and lost, living by values new and false; but their false values were at that time so much my own that I was blind to Hardy's meaning. How tragic, I thought, that Jude could not go to Christminster to be educated. I did not see what Hardy saw, that Jude, one of the last stone-masons, belonged far more integrally to the cultural inheritance of England than did the string of nonentities who, for him, represented the Oxford to which he aspired. To me, it seemed perfectly natural that Sue, an 'educated' school-teacher, should cling to those ridiculous plaster statues which for her represented culture; for I had done the same myself, with my Medici prints of *Primavera* and Leonardo's head of Christ. To me the tragedy was not the tearing up of the roots of Jude and Sue, which turned them adrift (always uneasily in the country going for walks or looking for lodgings or selling up the old cottage whose life must now become extinct; and not, like Tess, milking the cows or like Marty and Giles, planting the trees), but their failure to achieve what they longed for— and I also had longed for, and was now more fortunate than they in achieving: entrance into Christminster. I did not see, as Hardy saw, that the same misguided aspirations (or in-evitable process) would turn thousands besides Sue and Jude into displaced persons; into Lawrence's characters, without caste or orientation, who are but Sue and Jude a

27

generation later. I could not see this; for in truth I was myself one of these, an unconscious part of that same social revolution, its dupe and victim as they were. But I did know that Hardy had a vision of the mysterious greatness latent in human beings, and that Lawrence's people lacked that stature imparted by the earth itself to those who have not broken the ancient ties that bind Hardy's people to hill and wood and pasture. Not all my ties of the heart with Northumberland's bleak moors had yet been broken.

With Proust I did better; I read six or seven volumes in the original French, partly as a gesture towards M. d'H and Brittany, where I had been happy, where I had caught unawares a breath of that quality, that atmosphere of French culture which Proust so nostalgically evokes. The Bay of Concarneau, Pont L'Abbé, and the savage rocks of Penmarch, I too had loved. Because I did not realize how little French I knew, I persisted, and began to learn the language I pretended to know; and also to learn a little about society; for Proust's world seemed to me to be a living society (as, in a simpler mode, Hardy's was); whereas Lawrence seemed to be describing rather a lack than an actuality, less a way of life or a culture, than the embarrassing spectacle of people who have none; a breakdown of social order and orientation, or the rise of the outsiders, as one may choose to look at it.

I also set to work on *Ulysses*, then an exciting banned book. As with Proust, I would not admit, even to myself, that I found much of it incomprehensible; so I persisted from beginning to end. But Joyce I found here and there rewarding and full of a poetry whose beauty moved me. This, I was given to understand, was not at all what I ought to have found in *Ulysses*; what I should have admired was not the refrain of *Liliata rutilantium turma circumdet*, reminiscent of Roland's incense-intoxicated religious enchantment; nor the poignancy of Stephen's mother 'folded away in the memory of nature, with her toys'; no, it was the 'difficulties' of the style (an obstacle-race for clever intellectuals) and the obscenities, which were supposed to 'liberate' us from the restrictions of bourgeois morality, religion the drug of

28

the people, etc., etc., etc. All forms of disintegration of morals, social order, language and religion were indiscriminately acclaimed as progress towards that freedom of anarchy which was the vague utopia of the rebels of my generation. (This programme suited me well enough; I had after all, my private score to settle with Ilford and the Wesleyan Methodists.) Yet I admired in Joyce rather what he had in common with Synge and Colum and Yeats and AE; the vilanelle *Are you not weary of ardent ways*; the depth of family feeling; the Celtic melancholy music and beauty of language; and the resonances of the great culture of the Catholic religion; the warp of Ireland upon which he wove rather than the woof he wove upon it.

I had hitherto looked in poetry for the sublime, listened for that resonance of 'the eternal, in and through the temporal' of which Coleridge speaks; but I was now entering a world for which there was no eternal; a literature of the temporal was what in Cambridge I encountered, a literature compatible with Wittgenstein's and Russell's new logical positivism, Bloomsbury humanism (represented in King's College by Maynard Keynes and G. Lowes Dickinson) and the materialist science of the Cavendish laboratory, that power-house that dominated all fields of Cambridge. All was of a piece, the new taste and the criticism invented to justify it. There I discovered that the beauties I had hitherto found in Milton and the Romantics were not of the imagination, but imaginary; it was I who had failed to understand that where I had thought I had seen beauty, there was none. I and my simple kind had not the courage to retort that, if this be so, there is more value in the illusion than the reality; still less that to have seen beauty, to have been moved by feeling, is a fact which cannot be argued away. Better to have been moved by a 'bad' poem, a melodramatic or sentimental story, than to have missed the experience of wonder and delight. Holy personages have appeared through the vehicle of ill-painted icons, and worked upon those who so beheld them miracles unknown to those critics who seem to grow, in the long run, incapable of being moved by anything so simple and so beyond reason as beauty of any kind at all. 'The best of this kind are but shadows, and the worst no worse. . . .'

In discarding my own intuitions in order to learn a more 'intelligent' way of reading poetry, I truly thought—or thought I thought—that I was taking the way from ignorance to knowledge. For the intellectuality of the beautiful, as the Platonists have known it, my Cambridge had little regard; taking complexity of wit for depth of meaning. The intricacy of Donne's conceits seemed of greater intellectuality than the music of Shelley. For the poetry itself must conform to the new values of science—the quantitative and the rational. I knew nothing of the alternative and excluded culture of the Platonists; the names of Plotinus and Thomas Taylor the Platonist, not to mention Coomaraswamy, contemporary though he was, were at that time unknown to me. Nor could the crude form of Christianity known to me have withstood the scientific culture of Cambridge, complex, coherent, exciting as it was, even had I been trying as hard to retain it as I did to free myself from it. Yeats's *Autobiographies* I later read with secret joy; but I did not dare to say that his words seemed to me to speak with the voice of life in a world of mechanisms; to admire Yeats was not the thing at all.

It was after I had left Cambridge, but before I had begun to question its values, that I remember T. S. Eliot saying that he greatly admired Yeats's *Autobiographies* because these told of just those things which were important to poetry (or did he say to *the* poetry—Yeats's own. I wish I could be sure, for the difference though slight is important); and that too was one of the moments of intellectual liberation which I remember; my secret, unspoken delight was justified in the judgement of our great poet!

Hopkins too I now encountered for the second time; but how different was this Hopkins of Cambridge, this Hopkins of 'sprung' rhythm and hard-to-decipher syntax from Roland's Hopkins who had swayed a young man with half-morbid religious emotion! With vivid intellectual excitement, Cambridge (dismissing the priest's preoccupations as merely accidental) analysed the structure of verse and image; while I. A. Richards's friend, C. K. Ogden, tried to master the metrics of sprung rhythm. I was taken to visit him (I think in London, but I am not sure) and I remember how Ogden set a great humming-top to spin on the stone floor of the hall of his house until it sounded a level note; to which he chanted, first some odes of Horace ('*Faune nympharum fugientum amator*' was one) and then Hopkins's 'Yes, why do we all, seeing of a soldier, bless him' etc; a fine donnish performance in a vanished fashion. Many years later, during the war, for a third time I was to hear Hopkins read; this time by Robert Speaight, and neither as religious propaganda nor as an exercise in syntax and metrics, but, simply and superbly, as poetry!

The Imagism of the new American poets reached Cambridge in the early works of Eliot and Pound (and also H. D., Richard Aldington, and other forgotten names) and, in the context of the 'scientific' criticism of I. A. Richards, at once helped to create the new taste, and satisfied it. *Haiku*, as it were, without the Zen metaphysics.

I did not myself realize the paradox of my situation; for so strong in me were the associations of the very word 'poetry' that I went on trying to fit myself into that bed of Procrustes, believing that somewhere I should find, in the thought of this new school, what I believed must be there because they invoked the magic name. As to my mother the name 'West View' had persuaded her that a miserable building-estate must somehow still be a scene in Paradise, so did the name—'poetry'—mislead me.

Truth to say there was more of what I meant by poetry in my work in the botany and zoology buildings in Downing Street. There, among flasks and retorts, plant-tissues and microscopes and the bones of vertebrates I could still slip off my brave new persona and bathe in nature's healing stream. The marvels of the universe were there open to me and I contemplated in awe and delight the Book of Nature. I could think my own thoughts, arising unbroken from my

31

childhood's world of the Northumbrian moors, and perhaps from still deeper ground. As an anonymous student of natural sciences I was more a poet than ever among the Cambridge poets. There my experience was at once aesthetic and magical; those life-cycles and transformations, embryology and morphology, that condensation of force into form which produces sensible 'nature' constituted a harmonious world of significant form indeed.

Another world to which Cambridge gave me access—and for the rest of my life I am humbly grateful—was music. I could read music just well enough to enable me to sing among the second sopranos of the University Musical Society (then conducted by Dr. Rootham) Bach's B-Minor Mass; Vaughan Williams's *Sea Symphony*; Kodaly's *King David*. In the Madrigal Society (conducted by 'Boris' Ord) we sang, besides the English madrigals, Monteverdi and Vivaldi. In King's College Chapel mine was one among the young voices whose 'linkéd sweetness long drawn out' was prolonged among the fan-tracery. Even in the Girton choir what exquisite old carols and canticles we sang! It is one of my greatest regrets that after Cambridge I let music go, and relinquished my humble place in that most sublime of all the worlds of imagination.

If Cambridge poetry had no magic in it, my generation found glamour to sustain our imaginations on the stage of Terence Gray's Festival Theatre. It was during my first term that, with my avant-garde friend, I bicycled for the first of many times to that magical place, in Cambridge yet not of it. More remarkable than the romantically dim foyer, the revolving stage, the elaborate lighting was—if memory serves as a guide—the imaginative impulse, strong and authentic, the aesthetic sureness of intent, by whose means, week by week, our own little rockpool was refreshed and replenished by the tides of the great sea. Yeats and Lady Gregory had dreamed of creating in Ireland a sense of national identity by the agency of the Abbey Theatre; and Terence Gray came near to creating, in Cambridge, a colony of what was at that time a living culture throughout Europe.

32

What made the theatre, in those years between the wars, so apt a vehicle for the spirit of the age? In Ireland, in Lorca's Spain, in the Prague of the Çapeks, the theatre was sensitive to every tremor, neither commercialism nor inane experimentalism had as yet corrupted the impulse which in those years made drama its vehicle. I knew nothing, of course, of this larger world; but that made our own theatre, for me, so much the more miraculous. I had been used to reading books in solitude, and my poetic dreams too were solitary. Poetic drama revealed unguessed possibilities of shared experience of an imaginative world. My imagination was at that time sustained, more than by any other influence except music, by the Festival Theatre. To this day certain scenes, sequences of dramatic emotion, with all their *duende*, live on in me.

How much of the magic arose from the fact that we of the audience knew one another and shared with one another, not as members of some anonymous 'public' but rather as the élite of our Platonic republic, a collective delight? We up in the gallery were absorbed, like the rest, into the palpable blackness of the auditorium, dimly lit, as in the lodge of some esoteric cult, by green light. We unfolded those programmes on whose cover a futuristic figure in the style of Edmund Dulac reeled backwards as though Atropos had at that very moment snipped with her scissors the invisible thread of Fate. With much rustling we opened the transparent page whereon we were able to read in the dark the names of cast and dramatis personae. As the reverberation of a great gong that announced the onset of the tragedy quivered through our nerves and up our spines, the rustling ceased and the curtains rose on Terence Gray's first production, *The Oresteia*. I do not remember who the actors were. Later many names afterwards famous—Ninette de Valois, Flora Robson, Robert Donat, Joseph Gordon Macleod—were to appear on those transparent rustling pages. But upon me, at that time, the dramatic illusion worked too powerfully to retain any human name. Whatever study producer or maker of masks had made of Greek

33

theatre or modern stage, upon my virgin ignorance the impression was as if that tragedy were enacted before us, the ancient figures, masked and buskined, captured in legendary time, for ever 'thinking the thought and doing the deed'. How much more real they were than any actor! Rupert Doone (later to become director of the Group Theatre) afterwards became a friend; but for me he always remained, somewhat, a young Bacchus in a leopard-skin, newly leaped from Diaghiliev's ballet. It was as if everyday dress and appearance were the dissimulation, the mask, and not that infinitely more real figure enacted in a painted scene. If the arts be not more real than 'real life', what is reality?

By whatever stage furniture or contrivance the magic was supported, it was no mechanism, no *trompe-l'oeil* which then enchanted us, nor even the skill of the actors themselves, so much as youth's desire to be so enchanted. For us the stage was a magical space, set apart as a dream is set apart, within which each of us could enter upon some inner world. At the stroke of that resonant gong, as the theatre darkened, we became as uncritical and as absorbed as spectators of a dream. And as in dreams we never know what scene may unfold before us, so, week by week, we were shown in some unforeseen guise, in some new aspect or situation, what riches, what depths, what strange and infinitely varied un-guessed regions lay within the dreaming mind. We did not so much feel, 'I would have acted so' or suffered so, as 'I acted so; I suffered so.' For to each it seemed that we alone, in our most intimate self, were the enactor, the conscious being from whose life act proceeded, and word arose to the lips of the figures on the stage. Young as we were, did we divine that our own lives too might be scenes enacted by some caste of mysterious beings manipulating us within the magical space of a human lifetime, set apart for the realizing of some one among the infinite number of the possible stories, the possible acts, of the one humanity? At the time we were not merely one, but all these people of the imagina-tion.

The mysterious beings, certainly, let us guess something

of their inexhaustible inventiveness, in character and situation, in humanity's infinitely various response to the few and simple themes of love and death. From week to week we saw, with the inconsequence of dreams, it might be Çapek's *The Insect Play*, or the revolutionary Expressionist *R.U.R.*; or *The Hairy Ape*, or *Desire Under the Elms*, or *The Hawk's Well*; or Lorca's *House of Bernarda Alba*, or *Rosmersholm*; and the gods alone know how many more dramas of passion or protest, anguish or aspiration we felt, for the time being, to be our own. I do not remember that then, as increasingly in later life, I ever refused to give myself to the proffered illusion, refused to feel 'This is I.'

It is sometimes said now that it does not matter what we see enacted on stage or screen, depicted in sculpture or paint or architecture, or sounded on our ears in music, because we can accept or reject at will. But can we? Do we not respond at a level beyond judgement? When we are able to judge, to evaluate by critical intellect, are we not already beyond the power of art? And was it not through the deeper influence of the arts, beyond the reach of critical judgement, that civilizations were created and sustained? To suggest that modern man is impervious to those influences which created Athens and Florence and Thebes and the Imperial cities of Pekin and Kyoto is not to say that we are more 'advanced' but that we can no longer feel, no longer respond to the powers of life. But of course it is not true; the lie is put about lest we should become ashamed of the images we feed upon, in whose likeness we choose to form ourselves. Blake knew that 'we become what we behold'; and week by week, in our little city state of Cambridge, we became, at least for a few days, or even for only a few hours, but in memory for ever, Agamemnon and Orestes; became those laborious dung-beetles with their pile; became the daughters of Bernarda Alba, or Strindberg's Hyacinth girl. Some inner being, thirsting for experience and for self-knowledge, was able to enter into every situation and emotion, while as yet remaining itself cloud-like and without personal identity.

But with the literary friends whom I presently made, the talk was all of technicalities, dry dull talk as it seemed to me, without the sense of wonder or mystery. I had learned at school the basic technicalities of English verse, and from my father of Latin; but these exercises in rhetoric, at which I was passably good, seemed to me unrelated to the living process of writing a poem. I may have made too much of the difference, but I still believe lyric form to be the outcome and sign of poetic exaltation and not a prescribed shape into which words may be fitted—Plato after all, thought the same. It is in the nature of things that the English schools begin with what for the poet is the end of an imaginative process, with the 'words on the page', to use a cliché of a later period. I listened, but not with my poet's ear, to the talk of free-verse and imagism and conceits. I have been comforted to find in the autobiography of Dom Bede Griffiths that there were others as naïve as myself, at Oxford if not at Cambridge: 'I had always understood it to be the function of the poet to see beneath the surface of nature and human life and to reveal its inner meaning. The beauty to be found in the poem was the index of the degree of truth and insight to which the poet had attained.' So I too had supposed; and even, in the words of the same writer, that 'the function of art is . . . to evoke the divine presence'. I now supposed that I must have been wrong. It never crossed my mind that these clever contemporaries might not have seen these things, which to me were self-evident; I therefore supposed that they must have renounced such a view of poetry in the name of some higher truth (that pernicious humanist 'honesty' which mistrusts all knowledge but that of the senses) and were seeing with the eyes of a knowledge greater than my own.

Now I can see that those of my contemporaries who had accepted, implicitly or explicitly, the current positivist philosophy had lost access to the wells and fountains of imagination and were engaged in heaping stones to seal the springs which might, had they overflowed, have swept away that sand-castle. Or were they, too, like myself, en-

36

gaged in a joyless pretence? Were we all suppressing our better natures in order to impress one another or to conform with current fashion? Feeling was not meaningful within the terms of positivist thought, and must be stifled.

I went to one or two of I. A. Richard's open lectures on Practical Criticism. I was too immature, then, to have benefited from them. I was, I vaguely remember, taken to his house, once, by William Empson; too overawed to take in very much; and remember chiefly the strange impact of the Japanese *No* masks hanging on his walls. I have since come to know Ivor and Dorothea Richards as friends; and we share a love of Coleridge, Plato and Shelley. Ivor is a critic who, falling in love with the texts he studied, took to poetry; a splendid example to set against those poets who, led astray by the magpie criticism, become critics. I remember a lecture he gave, years later, at the Institute of Contemporary Arts, in London, on the *Ode to the West Wind*; ingeniously illustrated, as I remember, with little drawings on the blackboard of electric wires and switches and boxes, meant to represent 'communication'; from, as he said, an unknown source, to an unknown recipient: a process beginning and ending in mystery. Shakespeare would have done it with airy sprites, Blake with angels. The little diagrams were the vestiges of a style by whose disguise, in the 'twenties, it was necessary at least to appear to be 'scientific'. But the thought was metaphysical and Platonic.

Whether Cambridge did me as a poet irremediable harm, or good in the long run, it is futile to ask. I was bound to encounter in some form the climate of opinion, the current beliefs of the world into which I was born. Perhaps I am able now to speak with more authority on the side of Plato and Plotinus for having lived in, and through, the other culture. Not that I clearly recognized that I was involved in any such conflict of values, felt but not defined. What was at issue was Job's and Oedipus's question, 'What is man?'; and in the Cambridge of those days the materialist view prevailed. With greater knowledge I would have understood that two

37

irreconcilable systems were in conflict; but that realization presupposes greater knowledge of both alternatives than I then possessed. As it was I encountered piecemeal situations in which my foolish head was in conflict with my not yet wholly corrupted intuition. But how else are we ever led, by degrees, by trial and error, to discover and to acquire the knowledge we need?

For the time being, religion and poetry perished together in the same ignorance; an ignorance eagerly adopted as knowledge; I readily believed that such true intimations as I then had were to be suppressed. Besides I was so thankful to be free from Wesleyan Methodism that I was glad to let God and the soul go. I had suffered too much in the name of the former, and thought I should be more free without the latter. This was not a mere kicking over of the traces, for I really did think that in adopting—as I then did—the materialist philosophy which seemed so compatible with the matter of science, that I was being intellectually 'honest' —the supreme virtue in Cambridge. Pavlov's dogs and their conditioned reflexes, Koehler's apes and behaviourism, I imbibed as a part of my scientific studies. To Freud I was attracted in part by the fascination of the idea, new to my generation, of an unconscious; and in part also because in revenge for my earlier sufferings I was willing to see parents put in the wrong. But I must confess that the raw sexual instinct of which Freud wrote seemed to me to have little to do with love, as I had experienced it and continued to conceive it, and to have few attractions. From my Jewish friend I learned that Marx had extended the materialist philosophy also into the field of economics, thus revolution-izing the world. Intellectual 'honesty' for the time overcame intuitive distaste and I swam with the other fish in that medium of Bloomsbury humanism, Freudianism, Wittgen-stein's and Russell's positivism, behaviourism, Marxism, Imagism, to which presently was added le Corbusier's Functionalism. It is easier to acquire the fashionable ideas of the moment than to acquire, by an essential culture or by deep and prolonged study, standards by which to judge fashions. The rootless will always be attracted, as I was, towards avant-gardism.

So I set to work to learn the sour new style. I saw one day on the Girton notice-board that a third-year student who signed herself Queenie Roth had some volumes of modern poetry to sell; I went to her rooms and bought from the future Mrs. Leavis those works she had decided were not worth keeping; rightly on the whole, I am bound to say. She obviously despised me for buying Humbert Woolf, W. J. Turner, Victoria Sackville-West's *A Land*. But I persisted and did better next time; because I was so ill-informed as never to have heard of him I had the pleasure of discovering T. S. Eliot for myself. I picked up a magazine called *The Criterion* on the table of a provincial journalist, whose son's guest I was, and began to read a poem which began 'Lady, three white leopards sat under a juniper tree', and was hypnotized by the strangeness of a new beauty; a lament for beauty defiled and dishonoured and unavailing, 'the single rose with worm-eaten petals', a threnody of renunication, of relinquishment of all the old sanctity and loveliness of the world, affirmed in the poet's sense of loss; in which I recognized my own, in which a generation recognized itself, far more deeply, God knows, than in any of our shallow affirmations. Returning to Cambridge I learned that the poet I had discovered was famous; and I recognized in *The Waste Land* the spiritual state of Ilford given its enduring expression. It was a shock to many of us, who in his *Waste Land* recognized our own world, when it presently began to be whispered that T. S. Eliot was a Christian; what to us was mere reality was to him the hell of Dante, the state and place of those cut off from God. We disregarded his theology; yet a generation saturated in Atheism, Freudianism and Marxism inhabited, as we inhabited no other poem, Eliot's *The Waste Land*.

CHAPTER TWO

Experiment

MY JEWISH friend was the first to discover the magazine *Experiment*, in whose first number were printed some poems by one of its many Editors, William Empson. I claimed to be a poet? Very well, here I must stand my trial by my generation. Through *Experiment* I entered upon my own literary adventure. I read the Empson poems and found them so extremely difficult to follow that I could be in no doubt that their author was far more intelligent than I was myself; yet to me it seemed strange that what appeared to be a love-poem should open with the line:

And now she cleans her teeth into the lake . . .

I was naïve enough to be repelled by this image, with its insistence upon a physical function, animal process, inappropriate (as it still seemed to my eighteen-year-old self) to the theme of love; which to me still seemed to demand some image of the soul's vision of the beautiful as reflected in the person of the beloved. Let me here say, since I use term the 'soul' very often, that I am perfectly aware of the possible alternatives, such as psyche, brain, drive, complex, ego, and the behaviouristic terms. Each of these, like the psychiatric language of neurosis, psychosis, schizophrenia, paranoia and so on, cannot be separated from systems of ideas, ways of regarding things implicit in their use. If I use the Platonic (and Christian) word, 'the soul', that is because for all practical purposes I regard the total view of things implied by this word to be truer, or at all events more humanly rewarding, than the alternatives. If that view is, by the standards of Indian philosophy, perhaps over-simple, it would introduce too many complications to attempt to use Shankara's terms, alien to my culture; even were I able to do so. And the same would be true of Cabbala and many other excellent structures by which we can assess experience. Well, in those days at all events I believed in the soul as that specifically human life in us of which the body is the vehicle. It seemed then self-evident that this represents our 'higher' nature, and no less self-evident that what passes in that living consciousness—that being in us which we immediately feel to be our 'I am'—is of greater import than our physical functions. The experiences of the soul, for good or ill, I still supposed made up the matter of poetry; and indeed of all the arts, these being the expression and the record of the soul's self-knowledge:

> Nor is there singing-school but studying
> Monuments of its own magnificence.

I remember the incredulity with which a Cambridge friend once quoted Alexander the Great (was it?) as saying that man is 'never less human' than in the act of sex. My contemporaries may not have reached the nadir of a later mentality which sees us as never more human than in this act; but were already on the way to that kind of Darwinian orthodoxy which regards man as no more than one of the 'higher animals' and activated by physical stimuli of different kinds both from without and within. I see very well now the force of that argument of Aristotle's pupil; for the 'nature' of man was, for the ancient world, precisely that wherein we differ from animal, plant or stone.

But Empson's line was indeed a true expression of the new philosophy I was at the same time engaged in imbibing; I had not yet understood that those who adopt some sort of Darwinian positivism must forego such opening lines as:

> Tell me, where is fancy bred
> Or in the heart, or in the head?

or

> Love bade me welcome, but my soul drew back

or
> Rose of all Roses, Rose of all the world

Even Edwin Muir's

> Yes, yours, my love, is the right human face

would have seemed to us embarrassingly naïve. But I was eager to learn; Empson was admired for his resemblance to Donne; he too very modern in mood when it comes to the physicalities of sex:

> Marke but this flea, and marke in this
> How little that which thou deny'st me is.

In this new poetry 'honesty' (in terms of the new premises of science) decrees not love but sex; in place of the dreams of the heart the 'facts' of physiology, these being 'real', the dreams not. But of course sex is itself only incidental to William Empson's theme; or one might say that the incidentalness of sex (or love) and the anguish arising therefrom, *is* his theme. When the beloved is no more than the surface-tensions and viscosities of a chemical compound of 98 per cent water (of which a textbook of the time alleged even the Archbishop of Canterbury to be composed; which being so of course so much for his beliefs—but then why not Marx or Bertrand Russell?) so much for that for which the soul pines. The beloved is 'That mud/ I have heard speak, that will not cake or dry.' The scientists of the Cavendish laboratory (so near to King's College Chapel and Trinity Great Court, but in how other a Cambridge) had set the problem the poets must resolve as best they could: to discover the qualitative implications of their new modelled universe. Of the editors of *Experiment*, J. Bronowski, besides (in his first year) William Empson, was reading mathematics; and the writing of poetry had in the Cambridge of the late 'twenties no necessary connection with the English tripos. I. A. Richards's attempt to make his literary criticism a 'science' was perhaps not so much a literary exercise after all as a response to the scientific ambience in which poetic imagination at that time and in that place found its excitement, illumination, or whatever that quickening of the pulse may be that tells the poet that here is matter for poetry. Even I was aware that poetry must take into itself, and so qualify, the knowledge of our time; find for the human spirit its orientation in a scientific universe new and strange, but astonishingly beautiful. In that context I could well understand William Empson's attempts to capture that strange inhuman beauty of the universe which in awe-inspiring recessions leads away from the human world into distances minute or vast. The anguish of that situation which dissolved the beloved into galaxies and surface-tensions was real enough. God knows.

William Empson's 'tracer-photon with a rocket's life-line' plunged into a strange cosmos, accessible only to intellect; and yet exercising upon our young emotions a terrible negative attraction, like a whirlpool or the edge of a cliff. Intellectual honesty seemed to demand that we throw ourselves over, and the rocket's life-line offered little hope of rescue. Empson's tone of despair contained by intellectual stoicism expressed a more than personal predicament. I too was under the spell of the new scientific universe. This seemed to me, at that time, the 'real' world, and the world of Yeats, Shelley and what had hitherto for me been 'poetry', a fairyland which I must relinquish in the name of that reality; the gods of *Hyperion* (I knew the poem by heart) were, I was now told, mere literary furniture, stood for no reality known to my new world; sorrowfully, but in the name of 'honesty', I let them go. For I did not then know the ground of the philosophy of the beautiful and of the soul, and was easily persuaded that those who wrote of such things were only decorating the surface of 'scientific' realities with pretty fancies. I was not blind and deaf to the wordless testimony of the beautiful itself; but what I divined only intuitively, the flat clever voice of Cambridge ('what exactly do you mean by . . .') could destroy with pseudo-logic.

Only many years later did I learn that Vernon Watkins had come up to Magdalene, William Empson's college; but had quickly realized that the spiritual climate of Cambridge was deadly to his poetry, and had retreated to his native Gower peninsula and the company of that supreme poet of feeling, Dylan Thomas. He had read the signs and made his escape. The Master of Magdalene had told Vernon he would regret his decision for the rest of his life; but he never did: the daimon's advice is never wrong. That is perhaps what I too should have done; but I had no nowhere, any longer, to escape to. The 'Kathie' of the Manse had been driven out of her hiding-place in the wilds, and Roland's Lyric Love was now an Eton-cropped eighteen-year-old undergraduate dedicated to a ruthless pursuit of 'scientific', which is to say impersonal and inhuman, truth. The only course open to me was to go on, for I could not go back.

The one or two poems I had written, during my first year at Girton, were of an immature and personal kind, in no way comparable in quality with Empson's already mature and original poetry. However, I sent them to William Empson; and in due course, to my intense joy, I was invited to lunch by the poet himself.

When I saw William for the first time, he was reclining upon a window-sill of his rooms in the first court of Magdalene. I remember the impression he made upon me—as upon all of us—of contained mental energy, as of a flame whose outline remains constant while its substance is undergoing continual transformation at a temperature at which only intellectual salamanders could hope to live. This impression of perpetual self-consuming mental intensity produced a kind of shock; through no intention or will to impress; for William was simply himself at all times. William came down from the window-sill and brought in the College lunch from the window-box where it was keeping cool (or hot). I seem to remember that there was another guest; but in any company William was the one remembered. Never I think had 'Bill' any wish to excel, lead, dominate, involve or otherwise assert power; he was at all times, on the contrary, mild, impersonal, indifferent to the impression he made to the point of absent-mindedness. Nevertheless his presence spellbound us all. His shapely head, his fine features, his eyes, full lustrous poet's eyes but short-sighted behind glasses and nervously evading a direct look (I always mistrust people who look you straight in the face) was the head, in any gathering, that seemed the focus of all eyes. His mannered speech too charmed us; those Wykehamical intonations slurred and stressed into a kind of incantation, even when he was not declaiming poetry; which he did with frightening intensity, like one possessed.

He was beardless that year; but on a long vacation grew his first beard (I think on a skiing holiday in Switzerland) which added to the daimonic energy of his appearance. His mother (I remember his telling us) had offered him ten pounds to remove the beard; and he had written her that 'since no one had offered him a larger sum to keep it on' he was obliged to accept her offer. So the beard went; but not the instinct for that mandarin form of barbarity, which did assert itself later, as we all known.

The Editors of *Experiment* never took me seriously as a poet, of course, although they all, in turn, looked me over. J. Bronowski ('Bruno') invited me to tea in Jesus College, and produced for the occasion a bag of Chelsea buns and James Reeves, another editor. Only a few years ago Bruno (whom I later met again on account of Blake, and saw frequently) asked me, in the friendliest possible way, what I *really* thought of my own poetry; he was paying me the compliment of crediting me with enough Cambridge intelligence to share his own low opinion of my work and giving me the chance to disown it. Not, indeed, that I have any exaggerated notion of my own poems; they fall far short of what I should have written, of what I hoped to write; but had they been better, Bruno might have liked them even less. William Empson reproached me, at a poetry-reading at which, by chance or by the innate pattern of events, he himself, Vernon Watkins and I were reading our poems, with having 'escaped from Cambridge'; as if I were a deserter. I think he was sorry, from pure affection, for my defection; but that 'Cambridge', an imaginative entity so real, to which he himself belonged and had in great part created, was neither my beginning nor my end. Bronowski, in a television interview following a series of broadcasts entitled *The Ascent of Man*, described those years in Cambridge as 'the time of my life'. Bronowski's imagination responded to the new thought which has become, now, a popular orthodoxy, or norm. The received opinion in our little circle, in those days was, in essence, the theme of his broadcast series; even many of the examples, many details, came back to me, as I watched that series with a strange blend of nostalgia for what to me was less 'the time of my life' than a fool's paradise; and realization of how alien those ideas, once so familiar and so zealously accepted, must always have been to me. But at the time I possessed neither the courage, nor the knowledge, of my intuitions.

My first published poems were praised by only two persons. One was Herbert Read, to whom a copy of the second (or was it the third or fourth?) number of *Experiment* was sent, and who, to the surprise of the many editors, singled out my poems as having some quality. This was the first praise I had ever received, and praise to the young is something more than a pleasure, it is as essential as water to seedlings. The other was from the Earl of Listowel, then Lord Ennismore (or was he during that year 'Mr. Hare', as he chose to become for a time?). His letter I remembered often afterwards in moments of discouragement; for he told me he had liked my poems and that I should go on writing in my own way 'and let your friends' advice go to the devil'; a strong and astonishing phrase, to me, thinking, as I thought I did, so much more highly of those friends' judgement than of my own. A heartening phrase.

Sometimes William invited me to meet him in London during the vacation. He probably thought I was pretty. I think he was, besides, quite simply loyal to all his friends in an undemanding, impersonal, quite uncritical way, just because we were there. So, taking the train from Ilford to Liverpool Street, I would meet William on the steps of the National Gallery, or wherever it might be. He took me to the Noël Coward reviews, and to the Diaghilev ballet; *Le Coq d'Or* I remember, and *L'Aprés-midi d'un Faune*. We walked

46

together among the oriental gods in the British Museum. Left to myself I would no doubt have strayed among the Elgin Marbles; certainly never paused before Bill's Oceanic 'supreme god in the Ethnological section'. Those flame-encompassed bronze Shivas, communicating the sense of motion in stillness of a perpetual transmutation, seemed to me then (rather than the more earthly and serene Chinese deities) the very essence of William Empson. I was one of the few to read his manuscript, lost during the blitz (not burnt or bombed but left in a taxi by John Davenport and never found), on *The Faces of the Buddha*. If I remember aright, one of the contrasts made between the figures of Christ and those of the Buddha was that, whereas it demanded supreme artistry to capture the Christ-like aspect, the Buddha's face itself (and not some symbol comparable to the Cross) was the icon of the Buddhist world; an aspect capturable in its mysterious vacancy by even some ignorant village wood-carver. That expression, written upon the void itself, exerted its power upon the poet of the new void of our world of photons. The sense of the relative, the impermanence, the unreality of the appearances opened by the scientific universe, was old in Buddhism before our civilization was born. It seemed to me at that time a perfectly natural extension of William's intellectual passion and intellectual subtlety that led him to consider the face of the Buddha. He was not religious, but then Buddhism is less a religion than a way of apprehending reality. Is it fancy that it was also with William that I visited the Chinese exhibition at Burlington House, the most marvellous art I had hitherto seen? If not in fact, in spirit it was William who led me there, for it was he who opened our eyes to the Far East.

By the time William reached China a newer anti-religion was already rising to power; and as the son of generations of soldiers and administrators, William concerned himself with the political realities of the world, and therefore with Marxism; though his intellectual poise and detachment would of course no more have committed him to the brash Utopianism of Marxism than to the finer subtleties of

Buddhism. All the same, it is perhaps necessary to an understanding of his subtle sense of the relative to read his poems in terms not only of a scientific relativity but in the flicker of that everlasting bonfire which gives the same fluidity to the dance of Shiva as to the smile of the Buddha. Unreality itself, after all, is itself only relative:

Not but they die, the teasers and the dreams,.
Not but they die; and tell the careful flood
To give them what they clamour for, and why.

Our claims to act appear so small to these,
Our claims to act
Colder lunacies . . .

William was well aware that the answers, no less than the questions, of our sciences were only that rocket life-line of human knowledge thrown out into the void; which he knew (as cruder minds do not) no increase of that knowledge would ever lessen.

Yet I think I learned more, in those years, from the inspired talk of Humphrey Jennings than from any other person. I see him, in memory, as an incarnation of Blake's Los, spirit of prophecy; whom in appearance, with his full flashing eyes and mane of yellow hair, he much resembled. Humphrey used to declaim, with 'the mouth of a true orator', long passages of Blake's prophetic books. Years before he made his war-documentary film of the London fire-service, *Fires were Started*, he would recite the passage which begins: 'I see London, a human awful wonder of God.' Unlike other of my avant-garde contemporaries Humphrey had the sense of wonder and of glory. He talked of Triumphs, of Gray's Progress of Poetry, of Inigo Jones. He designed the costumes and scenery for Purcell's *King Arthur*, one of the most memorable of Cambridge musical productions. While the rest of us were reading Freud, Humphrey was already reading Jung's *Secret of the Golden Flower*; he quoted from Lao Tze, and not only in Arthur Waley's translations. I remember after one vacation return-

48

ing to Cambridge, having at last made up my mind to put Rosetti and the pre-Raphaelites behind me; to discover that Humphrey was using all his eloquence to reinstate them. His mother was a disciple of Ouspenski; and Humphrey used to say of her, 'My mother thinks she has the key of the universe in her pocket; and perhaps she has.' Of that denigrating rationalist 'honesty' he had not a trace, making whatever his imagination touched seem always more, not less, than it had seemed before. In none of the many arts he attempted (he painted, wrote, made films, designed for the theatre) did he ever succeed in expressing more than a trace of that inspired quality which remains now only in the memory of his friends.

Humphrey was already married, as an undergraduate, to beautiful Cicely Cooper. She was tall, statuesque, and as silent as Humphrey was voluble. She had been a débutante, and her wonderful simple clothes were in the style of *Vogue*; which I first saw on her table. Her little white straw hats shaded her beautiful eloquent grey Irish eyes. She was everywhere accompanied by her fierce Pekinese dog. From Cicely I learned with astonishment that cookery could be an art. When she married Humphrey her parents cut off her allowance, and they lived in poverty in a tiny house in Round Church Street, made elegant by Cicely's taste and Humphrey's skill. Humphrey (partly French) and Cicely, a perfectionist also, had nothing about them which was not beautiful. One basket chair only, but the stripes of the Basque linen of its cushions were right to a hair's breadth. On her small housekeeping allowance Cicely would make not 'rice pudding' but delicious *gâteaux de riz*: no more expensive, but infinitely better. Humphrey painted with the perfectionism of fine art the flimsy walls and doors and the uneven floors of that little house where poverty itself was immaculate.

It was Humphrey who made us aware of contemporary movements in France, who opened to us the pages of *Minotaur* and *Transition*, and *Cahier d'Art*. Later he became involved in the Surrealist movement and the friend of Magritte and Paul Eluard. He held forth on Marcel Duchamps and other makers of the movement of *Surréalism au service de la revolution*; under whose banner he harangued the young men of our new age. On whatever subject Humphrey held forth he was irresistible. 'You must *be* 1932,' I remember his proclaiming in that year; and indeed he 'was' 1932, following Rimbaud's injunction (often on his lips), '*Il faut être absolument moderne.*' It was from Humphrey we caught that magical awareness of the growing-point of the consciousness of the world, which is (or so we then believed) the poetic vision itself.

I know of no name for the phenomenon by which, in any generation at any University, the young discover and recognize in one another those who make up that mysterious growing-point. It is not necessarily those with the most distinguished academic careers who constitute that 'happy few' (we used Stendhal's phrase unashamedly, for it had not occurred, then, to anyone to call in question the self-evident existence of that élite). Not all its members were friends, or liked one another; but all were aware of one another. What strikes me now is how right were those instinctive recognitions and how many of those of my own generation were to become more or less famous. Aloof, in Trinity, Steven Runciman and Anthony Blunt; in Magdalene, Bill Empson, and the photographer Henri Cartier-Bresson; Michael Redgrave; T. H. White (author of *The Once and Future King*), was already respected, for he had published a little volume of verses, *Loved Helen*. J. Bronowski already spoke in the editorial plural—('*we*' think, etc., later justified by popular acclaim; to which, neverthelesss, he never sacrificed certain principles of intellectual and moral integrity). James Reeves; George Reavey, Pasternak's first translator; several young Trevelyans (I knew only Julian, the painter, at that time); Robin Darwin; Richard Eberhart, our American poet; in King's Julian Bell, killed in the Spanish Civil War, but not forgotten; Alistair Cooke, elegant with his bow-tie, about to take off for America. What we recognized in one another was not academic distinction, or any tangible achievement, but rather a sense of being involved, individually or collectively, in the advancing frontiers of, not so much knowledge in the abstract, as the consciousness of our generation. We felt ourselves to be a growing-point even when we were in the bud. This must be a natural process, repeated in Athens, Florence, Paris, Nalanda, Kyoto, Boston, wherever the Good City may reappear; as it will always reappear.

We knew fairly accurately how we ourselves and others stood years before we had been put to the proof. But I wonder how many of us realized then that Malcolm Lowry, the only one (besides Humphrey) of my then contemporaries to whom the word genius can be truly applied, possessed that gift of which Cambridge values took little cognizance? True, John Davenport, then as later remarkable for his discernment (he was also one of the first to acclaim Isaak Dinesen and a boon companion of Dylan Thomas), loyally and constantly, if prematurely, proclaimed Malcolm's greatness. He did indeed publish extracts from his first novel, *Ultramarine*, in *Experiment*; but it was only after many years that *Under the Volcano* showed us who Malcolm really was. Shy, tongue-tied, gauche except when he played and sang to his ukulele, little use at examinations, his gifts were of feeling and imagination; aspects of life little valued in our Cambridge. William Empson, among us in the full blaze of his glory, impressed us more, because his gifts were within the range of our understanding. William was able brilliantly to articulate a student's intellectual and emotional experience. As between William's brilliant gift of discursive intellect and Malcolm's inarticulate, profound feeling and intuitive insight, William's, at that time, impressed us more. Or must I say, impressed me more. Impressed me in part because William's brilliance frightened me and made me feel inferior; whereas Malcolm did not frighten; he was too shy, too vulnerable, to overawe; too disarmingly simple when he sang:

> This year, next year
> Sometime, never,

Love goes on and on for ever.
What makes the world go ro-ound is love.

Yet the singer of these simple sentiments possessed virtues
and qualities of genius that were no part of our Cambridge
scheme of things; Bill had no great opinion of him; and, as
always, I followed my foolish head instead of the simplicity
of that other faculty to whose recognition the head has, in
the long run, to bow.

I was in a sense committed to this world whose values and
whose philosophy, whose poetry and whose criticism, I
have since slowly unlearned. I had eaten in Cambridge the
pomegranate seed that in Ilford I had refused, and I was a
willing captive—was, indeed, captivated—yet in another
sense it was all unreal, my thin brittle new personality playing its part as in a play, or a dream. I played my part but did
not live it; yet I assumed it with, I must confess, much
enthusiasm. I was not, at that time, anyone or anything
except the part. I was I think entirely absent from myself,
and lived in my new *persona*; my chief occupation during
these years—my chief pleasure as well—was the constructing of one. I was a living example of those theories of
behaviourism and conditioning which I studied in my text
books. Heaven knows I had need of a mask, if only for the
protection of my interior self; but somewhere between
Ilford and Cambridge I had lost that self; lost my soul. Yet
that mask has remained the only one I ever succeeded in
constructing. I wear it, even now, with deceptive ease; for a
mask is a protection, a concealment. It is also uncommonly
hard to get rid of, like accent in speech, or other marks
written on us as we go through the world, which tell
strangers where our journey has led us. I have a great dislike
of my own mask, whenever I catch a glimpse of it. It fits
remarkably ill the person who slips it off whenever solitude
permits; yet I cannot disown it, it is what I chose to make of
myself, at that time.

I see now that my will and my heart were at fault or I
would never have been betrayed into ways of thought so

52

destructive of feeling. Heartless and hard as I was, with my little dangerous knowledge, I was a monster indeed. But what other ground had I, at that time, upon which to build a life? It was by no will of my own that my roots had been torn out of their native soil. There was no turning back.

There is one memory whose reproach has never left me; doubtless it is the symbolic veil of much more that lies behind it. At the end of I think it was my first term at Girton, my Girton friends and I planned to bicycle back to London, leaving our luggage to follow by Carter Paterson. The return to Ilford from Cambridge was, for me, like an extinction. The two worlds, the two lives were, in my experience, utterly unrelated: the one a nightmare which might after all prove real and swallow me back into itself; the other a reality which might prove a dream and elude me. Both could not be true. I do not know how to describe, except to those (and they must be many) who have also known it, the gulf which separated the two worlds between which my life was now divided. To my friends, home and Cambridge were only separate places in the same world, and life; to me they were as removed as the Tower and the Court to Calderon's Segismundo (whose nobility and whose philosophy I, however, lacked). I dreaded the end of term, the vacation which condemned me to become again my Ilford self. And yet my parents looked forward, and especially my mother, to the return of her spoiled beautiful clever daughter, as her own one slender link with the bright world. My mother's life was, I think, vicarious, lived through me; all that I was now living in that remote world she now hoped I would give her; while I, possessing a foothold of escape so precarious, feared above everything the intrusion of my parents upon my new identity, whose separateness from them I was determined this time, and at all costs, to keep. I had not survived without mutilation their destruction of my first love, and this time I was all defence. But to my mother I was herself, an extension of her own life, as Persephone of Demeter; but the roles were reversed, for it was my mother who was imprisoned in Hades, realizing
53

only in me, who lived in a brighter world, her dreams and hopes. But I was neither willing nor able to rescue her from her place of darkness, the scene, for me as for her, of so much sorrow. I feared to be dragged down myself and I saw no possibility of saving her from drowning. Her grief might well have drowned me, had I loved her; but instead, her love, her attempt to enter wholly into my life, I called 'possessiveness'; a fine word, scientific and unfeeling, from my brave new world. I had no mercy.

And so from my bicycle I alighted outside West View in a mood of guarded and resentful hostility. The house seemed smaller and uglier than I had remembered. Between the garden gate and the front door I had to shrink back into those mean dimensions which had once held me, and in which I had so chafed for freedom; to cease to be that wonderful winged creature I thought I had become; to become again my mother's Kathie, my father's daughter. The process was too sudden: the dining-room seemed to me unbelievably small, everything in it ugly, from the net curtains to the roll-top bureau and the black marble clock on the red marble mantelpiece. I looked round the room in vain for some beautiful thing upon which to rest my eye, and found none. But my mother had prepared for my coming; all had been dusted and polished with love. In the middle of the dining-table, on the blue chenille table-cloth, stood a vase, a blue and white vase of cheap Chinese ware; in it was a spray of mimosa. My mother asked me if I did not think it was beautiful; and, God forgive me, I said No. I repulsed her, and refused the flower she offered me. Now I cannot see mimosa or smell its heavenly fragrance, without seeing the blue vase, with my mother's flowers, and knowing that many murders have been less murderous than my cruelty then.

My secret intention, at Cambridge as formerly in childhood, was to be a poet; but what had I to prove my claim? My poetry, as I alone believed, lay in the future. And supposing I had been able to prove myself a poet (as William had already done) what do poets do, on going down from

Cambridge? Write poetry? But where, in what circumstances, in what capacity? I had no idea. I saw Julian Trevelyan setting off for Paris to be a painter, and this seemed right and natural. He lived there very simply—or it seemed simple. Julian Bell could live in the country, in his mother's cottage, and 'write'; and this too looked simple; the very name 'cottage' suggested simple poverty. Brought up as I had been to think that money did not matter, it never crossed my mind that the only thing which prevented me from doing likewise was the five hundred pounds a year on which each of these friends could afford to live simply. I early made a kind of vow to myself (I have even kept it with some lapses) never to do for money anything which I would not do for its own sake. I have in fact lived most of my life as if I had an income, without having an income. Most of the poets I have known have done the same, more or less, and survived by miracle. Now, believing as I do that all is miracle, I wish that my faith had been greater.

I had never clearly thought about the difference between a vocation and a career, or the practical problem of how to relate the two. I had not thought about a career at all; I had merely floated on the crest of the waves, never doubting that the world would somehow look after so bright a creature as myself. I had worked hard enough during my first two years and taken my Natural Sciences Tripos, Part I at the end of that time, thus becoming qualified for my honours degree. I had hoped, but not with much confidence for a first, and obtained an honourable enough II.I. I had therefore a year to spare, as it seemed to me; and at this stage the obviously wise thing for me to have done, had I been a sincere scientist, would have been to take Part II in either Zoology or Botany. Ill-advised—unadvised, in fact— I thought I could at this stage best be about my daimon's business by reading Moral Sciences Part II. I imagined, naïve as I was, that from 'philosophy' I should learn the deep truth for which I was ever in search. Under the illusion that 'psychology' would unlock to me the secret knowledge of the soul, of consciousness, or at least the material of Freud and Jung, I wasted a year in the Department of Psychology, which was in fact concerned only with the physiology of the sense-organs; I had strayed unawares even deeper into the mirk of behaviourism. I obtained only a third class in this ghastly subject; but I deserved no better, for my third year I devoted, in reality, to my literary education; that is, to the reading of Proust, Joyce, Eliot, Arthur Waley's translations from the Chinese, Greek drama, and a general course of English and French literature, ancient and modern, undertaken by myself with advice from my friends. I have always worked hardest and best at self-imposed tasks. As my father would have no priest between himself and God, so I would have no intermediary between myself and my fellow-writers; for so, from the very outset, I regarded them.

When, therefore, Cambridge came to its sudden end, I had no idea what I would or could do, and had no idea where to turn for advice. This may seem strange; but I had lost touch with those concerned with me as a student of biology, and my adventure into the Department of Psychology had been disastrous. In any case, what really concerned me was neither the one nor the other; and I was too much in awe of all senior members of the University to go for help to any adult. If there was at that time an Appointments Board, I did not know of it—this was not the sort of thing I ever knew. It may seem incredible that a not untalented student, for whom so much had been done, should not have known, at the end of three years in Cambridge, which way to turn; but so it was. My only friends were of my own generation.

Julian Bell took me to see Virginia Woolf to ask her to give me some kind of job at the Hogarth Press; but the tongue-tied, badly dressed, ignorant girl made on her (she looked worn and human at this meeting, without the *mana* of my first sight of her) no impression, and no job was forthcoming. I was interviewed by one or two head-mistresses of girls' schools looking for junior science-mistresses; but to them I was not Kathleen Raine the poet, but a young person most unsuitable for their staff, obviously not a lady, and only moderately well qualified to teach. The unbearable humiliation of these interviews threw me into a panic terror. For my father had meanwhile found a place for me as a teacher in a secondary school a mile or two from Ilford: I could teach there and live at home.

If, now, I were to encounter such a girl as I was then, I think she would inspire in me little confidence. I would not believe her capable of realizing a dream so remote from the circumstances of her birth and upbringing; I would be disgusted by her avant-gardism, would say, like the beautiful medical student of my first year, that is what comes of letting secondary-school girls into Girton: they lose their heads and their bearings. But it was not so simple as that; for most girls, secondary-school or otherwise, who go up to the University want to follow some specific career, and are set on their way to accomplish it; whereas I wanted to soar, to be a poet, to live as a poet, to think the thoughts of a poet. I had not realized that Cambridge was no more a place where such a vocation could be realized than was Ilford. Was I mistaken, has all my life been only a long flight from reality, a refusal of the Darwinian virtue of 'adaptation'? Yes, but to what reality, to what environment, then, ought I to have adapted myself? Should I have been a farmer's wife in Northumberland? I might have been happy if such had been my lot. Or a city clerk's wife in Ilford? The mistress of a distinguished Frenchman? The school-teacher my father always saw in me? Aunty Peggy, dear schoolmistress of the children of Bavington, astonished me once, later, when my life had become even more entangled, by blaming my parents for driving me up the educational ladder; she, at least, knew that the 'Kathie' of Bavington was a simple, happy creature, who might have found her place in that rooted world among my old companions. What good had my education done me? None, in her opinion. But my destiny was otherwise. Those, besides, who, like myself, had seen nothing of 'the world' but its Ilfords are not likely to consent to the curbing of winged dreams to fit such a norm. I was more ignorant than I knew of the world and its many doors, open or closed. To me it seemed like a blank wall of steel, and the thought of going out into it filled me with a nightmare terror which I could never have explained to any of those friends and contemporaries for whom the world was *terra firma* from the outset. I had no place in it save one from which I must escape, as from the City of Destruction; home, my only security, was the place from which, above all, I must escape or perish. Like the legendary martlet, which has wings but no feet, I must fly because I could not come down to earth. Fly or perish; fly and perish.

CHAPTER THREE

'From Fear to Fear Successively Betrayed . . .'

William Empson

PERHAPS I would never have accepted such spurious truths of Cambridge rationalism had I not closed my heart; which could never have been deceived by the new doctrine that 'honesty' consisted in disregard of feeling (which was 'purely subjective') in ourselves and others: a quantitative, positivist honesty. Pithed frogs, a charming dog made to run before Professor Barcroft's class of physiology students with the spleen stitched outside its skin, and many other things of the same kind caused me not a qualm, since the pursuit of that inhuman 'truth' justified all. Feeling is at a disadvantage when it argues its truth against that of cold reason. In the Cambridge of the 'twenties this was the more so because the scientific materialism generated in the prestigious Cavendish Laboratory and its encircling power-houses made reason itself serve the quantitatively verifiable. 'We do not cry because we are sorry, we are sorry because we cry'; mind is an epiphenomenon of the brain, love of sex-hormones, and so on. I do not wish to vindicate myself by blaming the mental climate of Cambridge; but I must say that spiritual defences stronger than mine would have been needed to survive. On the one hand the 'logical positivism' of Russell and Wittgenstein (then in their meridian glory), on the other the civilized arrogance of the Bloomsbury school, whose atheism was no less assured. And because between my father's unassailable puritanism and Roland's more spurious Anglo-Catholic aesthetic asceticism I had so greatly suffered (so I thought) through religion I was the more willing to join 'The Heretics' who met on Sunday evenings. Disbelief seemed, at that time, to offer a sort of freedom.

It is also true that the cold clear rational faculty, so able to wound, cannot itself be hurt, as feeling can. This, in the Cambridge of the 'twenties, was taken to be a mark of the superiority of rational judgements to those of the heart: the reason sees impartially, and is therefore unprejudiced. That there are matters in which reason cannot see at all nobody— if anyone dared to think so—ventured to say. Jung's *Psychological Types* had been published, but among the Heretics, Freud was orthodox, Jung heretical. I had learned my lesson quickly after making a fool of myself by confessing to a love of Shelley and Keats (William Empson did not approve of Keats) and of the Celtic Twilight. I had given a reading from the Irish poets at a Wesley Guild not long before I went up to Girton, but I soon learned not to mention AE and Padraic Colum and, for that matter, Yeats, who was held in equally low regard. 'The Early Yeats', they later called him, justifying their own failure to identify him as the greatest poet of this century; as though the author of *All Souls Night* were a different person from the author of *Fergus and the Druid*.

Yet prepared as I was to be heartless and 'scientific' towards others, I was myself agonized, guilt-ridden, and as sensitive as if some vital organ in myself had likewise been exposed to every painful touch. No woman is more dangerous to others than a young girl whose heart has been destroyed; as, between Roland and my father, mine had certainly been. It never occurred to me that I could be dangerous, for I was aware only of my own misery. When we are unhappy it does not occur to us, so much do we feel ourselves to be the victims of the world, the sufferers in every situation, that in our very helplessness lies our power to injure others.

The injury I had myself suffered through my first experience of love was apparent to no one but myself. I came and went in that young world, myself young, with enough natural beauty for my ignorance of how to behave or dress or float or steer myself (between excessive social fear and

60

excessive social elation) not to matter very much, buoyant with the superficial cold excitement of the unfeeling; for I, who had felt too much, now felt nothing, loved no one. I believed I would never love again, believed, in the words of a not-yet-quite-forgotten early influence, Fiona Macleod, that 'there is only the one love'; and for me that one love lay, I thought, in the past.

Yet I can distinctly remember once waking on a May morning in Girton (it must have been May, for the memory brings with it the scent of honeysuckle and the dapple of sun through young leaves) and the sudden surprise in which I said to myself, 'why, I am happy!' The leaden weight had lifted; it did not last, nor have such mornings returned to me so often that the impression of astonishment has ever been effaced.

Yet at the same time I did enjoy the power I knew I possessed; the knowledge that when I entered a college hall for some concert, or the foyer of the Festival Theatre, or bicycled down Trinity Street, or even took my seat in a lecture-room, I would draw, if not all eyes, at least a great many, exalted me the more pleasurably for my own vulner-ability. I do not say that I was beautiful (my bone-structure is plebeian and has not stood the test of time), only that undergraduates thought me so. I was told, half a lifetime after, that a little Society was formed to watch for me to pass, whose members counted the score each week of the number of times they had seen me. I do not even know who they were.

There was a time, in my first year, when Denis Arundel, seeing me afar off, was determined to give me the principal role in his production of Purcell's *King Arthur*; and for a moment I enjoyed, in Girton, the infirm glory of being 'the girl Denis Arundel was raving about'. (My father forbade me to take the part, pointing out to me that I was at Cam-bridge to work, not to waste time in amateur theatricals.) This turned my head completely for a time; for it is hard, at eighteen, to grasp the truth that to be loved for our beauty is not to be loved at all. We expect to be treated as the goddess whose reflected image we bear; we think we are ourselves that goddess. When at the end of my third year I had no idea where to go or what to do, William Empson's idea was that my face would adorn the cinema-screen and he sent photographs of me to his old school friend Anthony Asquith. The photographs were well received, but nothing of course came of it. I may add that I have not a trace of the actor's gift.

I discovered the power of my youthful beauty quite coldly, without happiness; and although I was quite unscrupulous about being admired at a distance, and fed upon such tributes, any closer approach threw me into an excess of guilt. I had brought with me to Cambridge, from my father and the Wesleyan Methodists, nothing of what was best in my father's morality, and may have been Christian in Methodism; but I did retain the strongest possible sense that to attract a man sexually must imply guilt on my part. I judged, besides, all professions of love by what with Roland I had known love to be, as deep as life. I had no other conception of it; that the physical instinct of sex could ever be separated from the depths of feeling with which, for us (and, as I still believe, for all the uncorrupted) it had been associated, I could not so much as imagine. To awaken such love, such tragic possibilities, must indeed be a grave matter. Twice I had brought sorrow upon myself and upon others by the inadvertent exercise of my power to evoke erotic love; and in Cambridge that power was all the more beyond my conscious control because I had become quite frigid; for not only was I pursued by my own heartbreak, by Roland's battles between desire and asceticism, but by my father's religious grief and anger, and my mother's tears—all caused by my fault.

So that, if other young women might enjoy the play of 'laughter-loving Aphrodite', to me it did not seem like play, but deadly earnest, guilt and misery. I tried to avoid and evade any sexual advance or entanglement, keeping the young men I met at the distance of friendship, trying to establish friendship. I was in this successful only with those of my men acquaintances capable of the kind of respect which friendship with a woman implies; or with men whose manners were good, and who therefore would never approach more nearly than they were permitted. It was, therefore, the very men I did not want and whom I liked least, those whose quality of feeling was least fine or who flouted convention, who were able to trip up my unstable balance. I felt myself to be like a creature hunted for its skin. I had lost

> The undaunted courage of a Virgin Mind
> For Early I in love was crost
> Before my flower of love was lost.

I hated and feared my home, I had no one to protect or advise me, my head was full of a confusion of untried opinions, many of them adopted for no better reason than that they seemed to offer me the greatest possibility of freedom from my parents' power over me; a sorry state altogether. Into this lamentable loveless, despairing helpless morass I sank deeper and deeper with every attempt to extricate myself.

For nearly the whole of my first year I kept my precarious balance; but M. d'H. was writing to me, laying his future at my feet and liable at any moment to arrive in Cambridge. This dreadful possibility I did not know how to prevent, for how could I be ruthless to my old mentor, my first philosopher and friend, towards whom I still retained the respect tinged with awe which children feel towards members of their parents' generation? While I was thus racked with anxiety a student many years older than the normal age of undergraduates suddenly 'proposed' to me. This was almost the first conversation we had had, for I had met him only as a member of the small biological tea-club to which I had been so proud to be elected, and so foolish as to imagine that my election had something to do with my promise as a biologist. His proposal took me utterly by surprise, his mature age put me at a disadvantage with him, but I thought I had, however badly, made it clear that I wished to reject his unwelcome offer. But, being extremely naïve and maladroit, I confided to this man something of my predicament with M. d'H. This proved fatal; and between my weakness and his want of whichever of the nobler virtues I had hoped or imagined I might have appealed to in him, I found that he had persuaded me into an 'engagement', and on that condition taken it upon himself to 'protect' me against my still honoured friend. What better pretext could I offer M. d'H. for ceasing to correspond with him than that I was 'engaged'? Thus I placed myself in the predicament of having blindly accepted the protection of a man I scarcely knew against the only wise and mature friend I had, then or for many years to come.

I distinctly recollect the sense of guilt and responsibility I felt at this declaration, although in fact such violent and sudden attractions have no more claim than has the moth to the candle.

My problem at once became how to rid myself of this man into whose power I had, through mere social maladroitness, fallen. He threatened suicide on my attempting to break off the 'engagement'; and I had not the discernment to see that this threat was most unlikely to be carried out. It took me more than a term to free myself; as at last I did by provoking a quarrel in which he himself requested the return of the engagement ring and the string of 'culture pearls' he had given me. I walked away from Emmanuel College, rid of these tokens of my degradation, like an animal which without knowing how or why finds the cage-door open.

It was after that escape from ignominy that I began to make those friendships among my fellow-writers which transformed my life at Cambridge from the obscurity of an anonymous science student from Ilford, to the infirm glory of undergraduate notoriety.

Brief as was that shameful and meaningless engagement, of one memory I cannot free myself: I took that intruder into my destiny to Bavington. In the summer vacation, he was invited by my parents to accompany us to the Manse.

No doubt they were thankful, after the sorrows my first love had caused us all, to imagine I had now found happiness, and as unaccountably welcomed this engagement as they had opposed my too early love. Of course he no more visited Bavington, in reality, than he was 'engaged' to me: both events were unrealities (though God knows such unrealities may swallow up a lifetime, not a matter of a few weeks only) for places have their inviolable secret essence, as have human souls. But that visit, in the degradation of that relationship, laid waste my sanctuary; I felt I could never, thereafter, return.

That miserable visit was to be the last time I ever stayed at the Manse; and now I was not able, any longer, to reach across time and what I had myself become and done, to my old companions and play-fellows and the fields and the moors; the well and the burn, the summit of Simonside on the horizon and the liverwort on the stone outcrop, the scent of camomile in the farmyard had, as Blake puts it, 'wandered away into a distant night.' Paradise was lost, but so lost was I myself that I had not even, any longer, as with Roland, the consolation of poetry; not even that grief which is still a mode of love, and a keeping faith with that which is lost. Where once there had been a place, and what once had been my life, had been myself, was only an apathetic negation.

To those who move from one social setting into another entirely different, the new world must always seem more or less unreal, dream-like; so that the natural proportions of human loves and hates, the sense of who and what we ourselves and others are, and how we stand in relation to them (things known instinctively, from birth, in any village, or in any world which is, village-like, continuous and hereditary) is distorted if not entirely lost. The child who in Northumberland had lived among people who were all, good or bad, clever or half-witted, part of the very texture of life, entered Cambridge after a period in Ilford during which, thread by thread, these natural attachments had been broken. Desperate to replace myself in the human world.

I was nevertheless almost incapable of doing so. Intellectually I succeeded, to some extent; but emotional ties are deeper, and do not take root so easily.

If I had not done it myself I would now find it hard to believe that an attractive and intelligent young woman, after spending three years at the most famous of women's colleges, could marry, as I did, without love, without sexual attraction, without any good reason at all. People may say 'but you must have *thought* you were in love'; but I did not: what I thought (if anything) was that I should never love again, so what did it matter? I prided myself upon making no attempt to captivate any of my more distinguished acquaintances— on having, on the contrary, held them at arm's length— the sense of honour of the poor, inherited from my father, and not, perhaps, to be regretted. But, with whatever scruples I had about what I would *not* do, I did far worse; not actively, but passively, in mere weakness; had I been, so to say, 'there', I would not have acted so: in my absence, these things befell me.

Where there is neither love in the heart nor wisdom in the mind, we seem as though involved in that blind mechanism behaviourists take the world to be. The sexual instinct is, when awake and living, vital, bringing together, for its own purposes, those who should be brought together, with much wisdom, so far as those purposes go. The blind passive involvement catches us up in a seemingly mechanical causality when, on the contrary, we are neither spiritually, emotionally, nor even physically alive; when the soul is inert we become like inert matter, driven hither and thither like the legendary atoms, by impulses which seem as if external to ourselves. Purposeless as the little balls that roll down pin-tables we are deflected on our passive, and always downward, course, by every obstacle; coming to rest in some pocket which may score five, or a hundred, or zero. The punishment of those who believe the world to be a mechanism is that, for such, this state exists.

The self-assurance and equilibrium of those who live on the physical plane does not exist in those whom nature designs for another kind of love. If the sexual instinct was at that time my undoing, it was not through its strength but through its weakness; no one who lives much in the physical could have been so overset as I was; what happened to my body did not seem to me greatly to matter, after my early heartbreak. It is not for myself that I am pleading the cause of that long-vanished young woman (for now what does it matter to me?) but for others like myself.

It was not, God knows, in the Christian sense a marriage; it was, rather, an alliance against society made by two young people whose only bond was a rejection of all those old values, good and bad, from which we were both in revolt. It was, one might say, an anti-marriage. I entered it with one secret assurance—that it would not last; it was an emergency measure. Neither believed in that old fiction of life-long marriage. Because of this tacit mutual cynical contempt for the marriage bond, it seemed not altogether like entering a prison, but, rather, like a kind of refuge.

But on my side there were more ignoble ulterior motives; marriage seemed a trivial price to pay in order to stay on in Cambridge, to go on walking among those trees, by that river, those buildings of beauty; and besides, I had no idea where else to go. My motives, then, were the fears and weaknesses of a character whose dread and ignorance of the world were limitless; his perhaps the 'bagging' of the white deer, or white blackbird, admired by many. But such prizes amount to nothing, when the excitement of the hunt is over, but a rotting corpse and a few feathers.

Upon such despicable grounds, then, I married. Love I believed was over; social duty had no meaning for me, since far from wishing to preserve the stability of the family and society from which I was in flight, my only wish was to escape. Despair, besides, does not rest in passive hopelessness, but is active, committing a piece-meal suicide in an impulse of self-destruction (or merely of destruction) which runs its course towards some decisive disaster, which alone can reverse the destructive process. It seems as if we are driven to make of ourselves and of our lives images of the inner grief and self-immolation of a broken love. The tearing of the hair and scratching of the cheeks is as nothing to the worse defacements girls in despair will work upon their lives. Despair is, theologically considered, not only a sin but the greatest of all sins; and yet at the same time there is a sort of pride in it, a pleasure even, as in the only great thing left to us. It is also a kind of revenge on those whom we imagine have driven us to it—in my own case, my poor father and mother, by now so bewildered by me. Their view by then was already that their daughter had broken their hearts and bowed them with shame in the eyes of their neighbours; and the terrible truth is, that this was indeed so.

Yet at this lowest point to which I had yet sunk, I had no conception of the nature or extent of the sin—to use the only true word for it—which I was so joylessly committing.

What we lived in was in truth fornication, not marriage, but just because we both so despised Wesleyan Methodism, because to us it meant so much less than nothing, cynically we made the blasphemous gesture; because a Christian ceremony could not touch such disbelievers, we were married (to placate our parents) by his father (a Methodist minister) in my father's church; in the Cranbrook Park Wesleyan Methodist church where Roland had practised Bach preludes on the organ, and two star-crossed lovers had gazed at one another entranced, through the sermons of the Rev. Edgar C. Barton. No one was invited: it was not that kind of marriage, there was no joy or love to share; and I went through it all as in a dream. I do not remember that I even thought of Roland; only now in writing of it years after do I feel the pang of grief for the violation of that early love. No one tried to stop me. My father had, I suppose, taken too much to heart the sorrowful consequences of his first interference to attempt a second.

Only one clue even then I did not relinquish: the determination to be a poet. Indeed a common intention to be writers was the only positive ground of our complicity.

The man whose name I so briefly, so inadvertently, and

so undeservedly, bore at that time, Hugh Sykes Davies, was a friend of so many members of our Cambridge literary circle that, in the matter of friendships (at that time a bond we probably both felt to be far more binding than that of marriage) our Cambridge life went on somewhat as before. Humphrey and Cicely Jennings were our friends; and Hugh was very close to Malcolm Lowry who came, like himself, from a Methodist background. Both played golf with the detached expertise of the intellectual and I have a vivid picture, more like a photograph than like a memory, of Hugh and Malcolm swimming together in Quy fen, while I, in a complex despair worthy of *Under the Volcano*, looked miserably on.

I had of course read the passages from *Ultramarine* published in *Experiement* and the book itself when it appeared. I was puzzled by Malcolm's evident feeling that the stoke-hole of a tramp-steamer and the brothels of Eastern seaports were somehow closer to 'life' than Monteverdi and Shakespeare played in College halls and the civilized minds of Cambridge. Not the point, of course—I missed the point. I did not understand that Malcolm had taken upon himself an exploration of the whole scope of his world, a quest for paradise which must take into account the hells, 'under the Volcano' on whose green and fertile slopes our Arcadia so precariously lay. We all thought of ourselves as the growing-point of our time; but whereas most of us were only the eternal avant-garde, Malcolm really was open to the suffering and heart-breaking aspirations of humanity's collective mind and most secret thoughts. For genius is not a personal gift but precisely that gift of access to the universal which Malcolm had and we had not.

And yet, though we did not know it, under Malcolm's volcano is precisely where we were, Hugh Sykes and I. I was his faithless 'Yvonne', though I did not, like her, in compassion return when I left him. Malcolm's book has, I now see, mysteriously defined the mental climate in which my first marriage had its brief existence. We were, unawares, experiencing just those underground influences, the subterraneous gathering of catastrophe that Malcolm Lowry so powerfully evokes. The uncharted freedom of a bohemian way of life, just because of its freedom from the ordinary social pressures, reflects, vibrates to, what is 'in the air'.

Hugh, like Malcolm, was very much aware of the Spanish Civil War and was presently to be drawn, like others of that generation (Burgess and Maclean were among his friends, as fellow-members of that élite of élite 'the Apostles') towards Communism. Herbert Read was related to him; and Herbert's gentle and idealistic form of Anarchism was a gleam of light in the sky over Dis, at that time.

But if we were living in the hells we did not know the place by its true name; this, we thought, is the reality of things, this cynical despair is seeing things as they really are. And the hells have their pleasures, if not their joys; not least among these, as Milton knew, the building of Pandemonium, city of those arts and sciences by which the lost adorn their doomed city. To give expression to despair, to uncover, layer upon layer, with the artistry of a Virginia Woolf, bottomless subjectivity; to strike heroic postures of bitterness; to fabricate opinions—these things have their joyless pleasure. We read Petronius and Lautréamont and *Ubu Roi*; and explored our habitation cut off from the light of heaven by the phosphorescence of Surrealism—soon to be *'au service de la revolution'*. Only Malcolm saw the hells for what they were; and in so doing—like Dante by the mere change of a point of view, under Satan's hairy thighs—was to be free of them, in the end, the volcano under him and the lovely light of Paradise dawning for him, at last, over the cleansing sea of Dollarton. But all that lay in the future. Neither Hugh Sykes nor I myself knew ourselves in hell, having quite forgotten paradise.

In secret my daimon still reproached me, but indirectly. I remember very little of what I did or thought about at that time, with the exception of the *No* plays of Japan, which seemed to belong, in some profound way, to that which I still was. I read all those translated by Arthur Waley, Pound and Fenollosa, and Marie Stopes. It was among the latter I found the symbol which at that time spoke to me: the play *Motome Zuka* (*The Maiden's Tomb*.) In that play the confrontation is with the ghost of a young woman who had, in mere vanity, urged her lovers to a rivalry which involved the taking of the life of a mandarin duck. Why this so deeply shook me I did not know; it is when we do not know why they move us that symbols have, indeed, power. There were some manadarin duck in the Cambridge Botanic Gardens; and their strangeness, like the idiom of an unknown, highly subtle and profound Eastern language, I pondered over. I felt the unbounded nature of the maiden's guilt and grief, more deep than that of the mariner for his Albatross, so it seemed to me. What had I killed? I did not know. Perhaps, hating and despising the human kind, including myself, I could be touched only by the innocence of animal nature, made to suffer by the evil of man. Perhaps I had some obscure sense of inadvertent responsibility, of what those do who 'know not what they do': the girl had not intended harm to the creature, yet her heartlessness had started a chain of cause and effect of which the death of that innocent beauty was the term. In her hell she reproached herself less for the rejection and death of her suitors than for the death of the bird. I perhaps sensed in that philosophic play a morality far different from that from which I was in flight, a morality cosmic and inexorable. Sin, in that perspective, does not consist so much in the deliberate act knowingly committed (the Church's 'grave matter, perfect knowledge, full consent') as in the state of ignorance itself. Unawares and even against the conscious intentions such a state of being may—indeed must—set in motion a series of fatal consequences. I did not know why the myth so held me; but I knew in myself those hells of emptiness through which the maiden falls and falls to all eternity. I knew, too, her perverse, despairing refusal of proffered salvation, her remorse which was nevertheless so far from repentance because loveless, self-enclosed, for ever cut off. Her cry 'This too I have done, this too I have done' spoke to me at that time as from the depths of my own life; yet, just as a child does not realize that the power of a fairy-tale lies in its truth to the archetypal nature of childhood itself, so neither did I recognize the power of *The Maiden's Tomb* over me as an identification with the maiden's guilt; still less did I see wherein her guilt (or my own) lay. I pitied and was aghast at her fate.

Only in reviving this memory thirty years after do I recall an earlier mandarin duck. In my first term at Girton I had bought for my mother on her birthday one of those prints sold at the British Museum, a Chinese painting of mandarin ducks and a lotus. (Years later I saw the same, or a very similar print in Mrs. Yeats's house in Palmerston Road in Dublin, and wondered under what circumstances W. B. Yeats—if it was he—had chosen that print.) Was my terrible sense of guilt occasioned by the knowledge that I had destroyed the deepest link of my childhood, that with my mother? That I had betrayed her, perhaps killed her soul, or my own? It may well be so. All that I had from my mother, the flowers of my childhood, Bavington, Scotland, everything I had ever loved and been nourished by I had betrayed and had cut my life off from hers, leaving her, as well I knew, desolate in Ilford. But nothing of that had weighed with me one straw in the balance with my own impulse to escape.

A Chinese poem translated by Ezra Pound I also used to repeat to myself:

> It is said that a certain princess
> When she found she had been married by a demon
> Took a garland of jonquils
> And sent them to her lover of former days.

Yet I no longer loved Roland, he was gone, forgotten, I thought of him without a pang. The charm the poem exerted over me was, so I thought, purely literary.

My despair, if such it was, was painless, for I was at that time dead to all feeling, and saw my guilt and my sorrow alike reflected in the mirror of symbols, as if apart from myself. I coldly watched myself as from a great distance living a life utterly unreal to me; as if I were someone else. I fell very mildly in love with a charming homosexual friend; this sentiment I felt to be innocent because sex and physicality were not involved. It was also a turning towards lost France (he was French). I saw in the kind of Platonic love possible between a homosexual man and a woman a relationship free from the squalor of the body, and vaguely felt that such a love would be appropriate to me. I had always, as a student, been attracted towards such men, who were, indeed, so often physically beautiful, and of a fineness of feeling lacking in the others, at least in their behaviour towards women. They did not hunt me for my skin, and I knew that if they liked me at all it could only be for myself—whoever she was. As to my body (as distinct from my beauty, which I thought of as something apart) my attitude towards it was of contemptuous indifference. It seemed no longer myself, or even mine. Like any prostitute I was able in this respect also to be what I would have called 'detached' —a cardinal virtue of scientific rationalism. Rimbaud's *je est un autre* was another of the phrases of that time; in a sense, however, far removed from the deeper meaning which I would see in it now. It was, rather, a kind of disclaimer of any responsibility for that detached 'other' who went through the motions of life bearing my name (or not even that, for I bore, then, the name of a stranger). Apathy is a kind of half-suicide, of all the forms of despair the most abject. When I was absent from myself I think I was capable of any degradation, nothing seemed real enough to matter very much at all. I wonder if the worst atrocities have not often—or always—been committed in the absence, so to say, of the person? Whether or not this is so, such absences are extremely dangerous, for those absent from themselves can perform any ruthless or degraded act with complete indifference; even with a kind of masochistic self-pity. 'That I should come to this!' we cry within ourselves, desperately hoping that if things become bad enough some angel or minister of grace will come to our aid. We fling ourselves downwards hoping to find ground if we sink low enough: there must be, we somehow believe, a limit to the fall.

I do not know how we may ever know, in retracing the record of the past, where our responsibility lies, and where we have merely undergone rather than enacted, lived through rather than lived, an event, unless by the sense we have of abiding identity with that past self, or event, or action performed, for better or for worse. I find, for myself, that this sense of identity with past selves is by no means continuous. It is rather as if at times I was present in my life, at other times absent from it altogether; especially after my childhood. The mind which wandered among the structures of mosses and lycopodia in the laboratories of Downing Street was certainly mine; but not the Girton undergraduate whom many of my contemporaries seem to remember better than I remember myself; nor the neurotic bohemian who so dishonourably prolonged her residence in Cambridge, which she dared not leave because she did not know where else to go, by the travesty of a marriage.

Yet up to this point in my life I could perhaps still have pleaded that I had been the victim of circumstances; monstrous as I was, I had in great part been bent and diverted from my true direction by people whose power over me was a part of the given conditions into which I was born, and which were none of my making. Some, even, of my most violent reactions may have been not the least, but the most excusable. But when does responsibility begin? Is it a gradual matter, or are there moments, confrontations with the powers of life, when we make choices by which, because we so deeply made them, we must abide? I believe there are such moments; and marriage ought, of course, to be such a deep choice. In fact this is not always so, and mine was not.

Which of my marriages, if either, the Catholic Church, for instance, would regard as valid, I do not know; it has long ceased to matter. If I were to meet, by the well of life, the Judge, I would say of myself, now as then, 'I have no husband'; and perhaps I should be answered, 'Thou hast well said, I have no husband. For thou hast had five husbands; and he whom thou now hast is not thy husband, in that saidst thou truly.'

74

I never, as a writer, relinquished the name my parents gave me; 'Kathleen Raine' has been my only enduring identity, yet even that is in some ways accidental; for the poet in me is my mother's daughter, whose name, Jessie, is mine also, although I have never used it; the 'Kathleen' was given to their baby by two young parents who thought it 'sounded better' (with Raine) than Catherine, the name of the aunt after whom I was named. Perhaps I was misnamed at birth; and that secret identity beyond the name? I have at times felt that I have no name, or do not know it.

But that nameless identity I have never relinquished for any man; and had I done so that would have been, I believe, a far deeper betrayal of an original and anterior dedication, one as deep as life, a bond with my daimon not to be broken. No relationship with any man has ever been, for me, of a comparable reality. I mistrust any kind of plea for an exception to the great and abiding laws of life; and yet the vocation of those dedicated to the gods has in all traditional societies been recognized; and the monstrous Medusa was a priestess who broke her vows. Perhaps for many people such questions as these do not arise; but I know that such a predicament as mine does, as a reality, exist. In a simpler world I might have been a nun, or temple virgin, or *devadasi*. I have had to discover, without guidance and with much pain, that my destiny is a solitary one.

Have I merely clung to the illusion that to be a poet was my vocation rather than face the appalling 'realities' of life? M. d'H had given me a phrase of ancient wisdom which as a schoolgirl and long thereafter I used to repeat to myself, like a *mantram*: 'Better to be a crystal and be broken than perfect like a tile upon the housetop.' I never doubted that I was crystal, though to be broken did not seem in any way inevitable; nor did I reflect that tiles are more fragile than diamond, for that matter. In my happier moments I have seen—I still see—the poet's vocation as heaven-sent. But was that compelling imperative secretly implanted in me by my mother who, before I could hold a pencil, wrote down my infant poems? In secret she summoned me to

75

realize her dreams, her unused gifts, her unfulfilled imaginative capacity for experience and expression. She, more naturally gifted than I, was bound by the conventions of her generation, the narrow circumstances of her life, her hawk's eye hooded in her captivity. Was the summoning voice her voice? Perhaps in part this was so. But supposing the sense of vocation—a human experience so universal—to be in part explicable in terms of Freud's 'super-ego', may not this in itself be an aspect, the appointed means, of the process of human aspiration carried on from generation to generation?

Yet in moods of despair, or perhaps of sober realism, a far different voice has mocked me; reminding me that, after all, my poetry has amounted to nothing of value and is no justification for a life whose mere selfishness has masqueraded as vocation. I can make no defence; it may well be so. And yet despair is only another and more destructive sin. Better to try and fail, I try to tell this mocker; better to fail than not to make the attempt. And then the accuser speaks his deadliest word: 'It is not only you yourself who has suffered, you have made others suffer, others pay the price of your poor little vain volumes of verse. I am only', he adds, 'here to open your eyes to the real state of affairs.' And I try to say, Shelley? Coleridge? Milton? Does not the great gift of their poetry to countless lives justify their catastrophic domestic stories? And at that the Devil laughs; for where is my *Prometheus Unbound,* my *Kubla Khan,* my *Lycidas*? Very well, I say, I deplore the failure, the betrayals, through want of courage, through cowardice, through whatever cause, of that clear calling. Was it not the man with one talent only who, in despair, buried his in the ground, to be condemned for his hoplessness? And without trying to write poetry I might have failed just as catastrophically to live a good life, caused and experienced no less suffering. Do only poets fail in the conduct of their lives? And is not every life a vocation (I say, my courage returning), a way to be followed truthfully, come what may, and not only the special case of poet or nun?

Let me, in all humility, own that, as regards marriage, I am of Shelley's party still. Neither the maintenance of social order nor the natural claims of the family have ever seemed to me of the same order of value, or of reality (which is the same thing perhaps) as the soul's pilgrimage, whether the pilgrim be poet or no. I cannot regard a life as a brick in a social structure, but only as a way, which each must follow, out of the mystery, into the mystery again; my most fatal dishonesties, from which have resulted injuries both given and received, have all come from my cowardly attempt to take cover within some social structure or institution. When I have realized my mistake I have without hesitation or remorse set about extricating myself. I never saw any reason to regard a mistake as binding; still less as sacramentally binding, but then sacrament was something, in those years, entirely outside my comprehension or experience. My remorse has been in all cases for entering, not for abandoning, untruthful relationships and situations. Heaven knows what moments of nostalgia I have had for that sweet lost paradise of the love between man and woman, the natural bonds of the family; but of those relationships, as it has proved, I was incapable. Having said all, I cannot justify, but can only affirm, my destiny.

CHAPTER FOUR

The Somnambulist

I ALLOWED myself to be rescued from my first marriage by Charles Madge; for this I was altogether to blame, for I was older than he, and I allowed him, in the chivalry of his poetic vision of me, to wreck his University career for my sake. He had fallen in love with me afar off; written poems to me. It seemed as if I were summoned by him with the voice of poetry. Did I love him? God knows; I was too desperate a creature for any sane or happy love; but I did see, as some Lady of Shallott might see in her glass, his nobility of character, his rare poetic imagination. What he saw in me, only God knows too; my delusive and neurotic beauty, of course; perhaps his poetic muse personified, since he knew me to be a poet; perhaps some Florimel fleeing through her night-wood of enchantments (Spencer was the poet he most loved; in appearance he somewhat resembled him;) perhaps, even, a woman of the people, whom as a Communist (as he had just become at that time) he could fitly idealize. Our relationship was altogether noble on his side; and even on mine there was cast a sort of reflected nobility. I remember well the terms in which he offered himself to me: 'Come with me,' he said, 'and I will give you a cause to live for.' What he offered me was the cause of Communism; and I, sickened by cynical hedonism, missing, perhaps, the Christian aspiration of my father's house, listened.

I was like an invalid paralysed by a mortal illness when he drove me away from Cambridge in his car; an illness of the will, invisible. I clung to him in the desperation of weakness, grateful beyond words. Yet I wept and wept and could not be comforted, imprisoned in my own selfish shame, as if it were my life and not his which had been ruined by our elopement. Once he drew a portrait of me on a handkerchief, a sort of Veronica's napkin on which he depicted a weeping face; which was indeed the face I turned to him. On the wall of the little room where we lived in Upper Gloucester Place he painted over the fireplace on the white wall, a tree with faces in it: the faces of our children, as he imagined them, and saw them in the glass of the future.

While I clung to him as a drowner to a straw, I was at the same time so ashamed of my elopement that I would see no one, and would meet neither my former friends nor his; for many months I hid from my parents. I seemed to have lost all identity. I would not, then, have dared to use my Cambridge degree in applying for any kind of post, for I felt I had forfeited all right to use it. For a while I hawked men's socks in the city; I tried to get a job as a manageress in the Lyons' tea-shops, but was rejected. I cannot remember what I then did it is all too terrible. Once I remember Charles had persuaded me to go with him to a party given by Janet Adam Smith in Ladbroke Square. I remember getting as far as the second floor landing seeing the former and future friends for whose friendship I longed through the door. There was an eight-some reel in progress; the first time I ever saw Edwin and Willa Muir, the merest fleeting impression for I turned back from that innocent happy throng as into the outer darkness of the outcast. On the landing of the stairs I wept, Charles striving to comfort and persuade me to go in with him; but I would not.

Yet his mother heroically accepted me and was more kind than I ever deserved. How she could have endured to let me set foot on the lawns of North End, under her ilex trees and limes, how let me enter that house where all was 'accustomed, ceremonious', in which she, a war-widow, had like a Roman matron brought up her two sons, sent them to Winchester and Cambridge, hoped for them—and of Charles especially—great things, by me laid waste, I cannot now conceive. And yet she did; she must have found my

79

commonness hard to endure, but she never for a moment made me feel that this was so; only once she asked Charles to ask me not to wear a beret for a hat. But I loved her; and this perhaps she knew. Had I been she I could not have behaved towards the intruder, the wrecker of a mother's hopes, as she behaved towards me. To the end of her life, every Christmas, she continued to send me ten shillings to buy some plant in her name. The one I think of as especially hers is a verbena; for in her garden there was a most luxuriant and lovely verbena, wrapped each winter in careful sacking.

Charles, perhaps because of its very perfection, because he had as a child and as a boy been so happy, was in reaction, like Prince Siddartha, against a life too perfect. From Winchester to Magdalene he had gone, the fine product of an old culture. (Charles's father had been one of 'Milner's kindergarten' in South Africa, where until 1914 he remained as a District Commissioner; as Colonel of the Warwicks, he was killed in the trenches early in the first world war.) It takes many generations to produce a house like North End, such women as Mrs. Madge, bred in those austere patrician values he was himself about to abdicate.

Nearly all Charles's Marxist friends were of the upper or upper-middle classes; there was one Honourable, and a number of Wykehamists whom he had magnetized with his own enthusiasm. They were the victims of the conscience of the English ruling class, as was Charles himself, idealists with nothing to gain and everything to lose by the revolution for which they worked all the harder for that, blinded by their own disinterestedness. Charles himself had never seen the working-class until one day the hunger-marchers from the northern coal-mines (my father's Durham) appeared in Cambridge, and he became a convert to the cause of such squalor and misery as he had never dreamed could exist. Charles and his friends in pure disinterested generosity were willing to throw away the heritage of their culture, of all that had gone to create their own sense of *noblesse oblige*. The crowd, 'the workers', they saw from afar off, and in the light of their own high level of

80

culture; and of such idealism as theirs, of course, the real revolutionaries were glad to take advantage. What none of these patricians of the Left understood is that what they were prepared to give and share would not be received but merely cease to exist. It was not a matter of more young men being given the 'opportunities' they had themselves enjoyed, the North Ends, the College cloisters, but the cessation of such things, which after the revolution would simply not exist at all. The masses will not even know what they have destroyed.

Meanwhile Charles conceived that strange half-poetic half-sociological expression of the pre-war years, Mass-Observation; he joined forces with Tom Harrisson, who had been studying the anthropology of Bolton and Blackpool. We lived, then, at Blackheath where we had gone to be near Humphrey and Cicely Jennings. Humphrey was working with the left-wing film-director John Grierson, and another Cambridge friend, Stuart Legg, in the G.P.O. film-unit, which at that time was making documentary films of 'men at work'; a pale reflection of the post-revolutionary Russian films of those years. To Charles, who seemed at the time a man inspired, almost as a medium is inspired or possessed, the idea of Mass-Observation was less sociology than a kind of poetry, akin to Surrealism. He saw the expression of the unconscious collective life of England, literally, in writings on the walls, telling of the hidden thoughts and dreams of the inarticulate masses. In these he read, as the augurs of antiquity read the entrails or the yarrow-stalks, those strange and ominous dreams of the years just before the second world war. This was poetry indeed; but to me the mass and its mind was terrible and deeply antipathetic; was, indeed, that from which I was in flight. During my calamitous 'engagement' I had attended, with that unwanted fiancé, the cup-final match of the Football League. There I had seen the crowd, many-headed and pullulating, its component units seeming scarcely human and its aggregate lacking any feature of the 'human form divine', its only language a roar. But to Charles, as to our as yet unknown contemporary Teilhard de Chardin, the soul of collective man was mysteriously beautiful. Once I remember we were walking together in Kew Gardens, and came upon a waste corner filled with single aster flowers. These flowers, with their many hundreds of solar discs, all turning to the one sun with the heliotropism of Blake's sunflower seeking after that sweet golden clime, seemed a symbol of the crowd, of the innumerable multitude of mankind, anonymous, equal, each imprinted with the same form, yet as a mass, in the mass, possessing a beauty of multitude beyond the beauty of any single flower, though each flower also had its unique and particular beauty. I saw the asters through Charles's eyes; as I did the writings on the walls of the great city, the multitudes of smoking chimneys between Charing Cross and Blackheath, and the rows upon rows of brick back streets all bearing witness to the human mystery. I tried to overcome my instinctive aversion from the Giant Polypus, and to see all this, as he did, not as sordid blind sub-humanity, but as strangely, mysteriously glorified, as if lived by a great life-force immortal beyond all those meagre mortalities in whom its stress and pressure was at work. The crowd Charles saw, as some other Marxist poets have seen it—as Edwin Muir once saw it in a state of visionary exaltation—not with fear and hate but with a participation almost mystical. As Plato describes the communication of poetic enthusiasm by the image of a chain of rings all magnetized, we all caught from Charles (for he was the magnet) a vision both high and prophetic.

Yet at Blackheath I felt always (as I told Gay Taylor at that time, and she later reminded me of the words) as if I were living in someone else's dream; and Charles was the Red King; in his dream I lived in a state of enchanted unreality. The unreality was not in Charles's dream—which for him was reality itself—but in my own state. I had strayed—trespassed, rather—into the life of another human being, not so much as a person who comes into a room where there are other persons, but rather as a ghost or a somnambulist ('Cesare the Somnambulist' in *The Cabinet of Dr.*

Caligari was a potent image of that time doubtless because—
and not all of them in Germany—there were many somnambulists) or as a spectre produced by the displacement of an
image by mirrors may seem to be in a place where it is not.
Never did Charles for one moment give me cause for unhappiness; I felt him then, and in retrospect see him still, as
a being of finer quality than myself. As a spectre might truly
wish to be part of the world through which it appears to
move (if a spectre could wish anything at all) so I could well
have wished to be really where I seemed to be.

Often in dreams to this day I find myself back at 6 Grotes
Buildings, the beautiful house we then lived in so precariously, between Charles's imaginative poetic exaltation,
and my tears and guilt and despair. There was a big almost
empty drawing-room where, alone, I used to dance, possessed perhaps by the same daemon that had once possessed
Zelda Fitzgerald; for like her I was desperately neurotic and
unhappy even while the dream possessed me; and only
while I danced did I seem free; 'dying into a dance' from my
distraught self. Charles let me dance, let me be free, let me
write. We both wrote, though he far better than I; concerned
only with our own poetry and one another's and with the
imaginative works of our friends, we offered ourselves to
the Zeitgeist, dedicated in mediumistic obedience to a mind
as it were outside ourselves, the consciousness of that
collective animal mankind.

We lived in a state of imaginative exaltation deriving in
part from Charles's almost mediumistic visionary sense of
the auguries and writings on the walls of those strange years
just before the second world war; and in part from the
infection of the French equivalent of the same phenomenon
of the rising towards the surface of unconscious themes.
Through Humphrey flowed the intoxicating obsessive
'paranoiac' images of the *Surréalistes*, the 'possessed' of
France. We were (in William Empson's phrase) 'waiting for
the end' in a state rather of exaltation than of despair,
as if the spectators of an unfolding cosmic drama. Dali
seemed to express the unformulated content of our own

unconscious state, a blend of brooding dread and somnambulist eroticism, passive, bewitched, yet also seeking, among the wreckage of the outer and inner worlds in which we were astray—worlds which had strangely and ominously converged, as if the outer, instead of offering us protection from our nightmare, had become possessed by it—some pearl beyond price which we felt to be just behind and beyond the veil of each obsessive symbol. In the sea-shell, in the fragment of broken pottery or wave-worn cork (the *object trouvé* attracted towards the waking dreamer as in sleep images less tangible but of a like power of magic arise before us), we hoped to discover this mysterious all-potent and world-transforming talisman.

The veils which concealed this potent marvel were sordid and sorrowful yet obsessively haunting. Mass-Observation, concerned with man, was essentially urban. We hoped to discern on the surfaces of dingy walls, on advertisement hoardings, or written upon the worn stones of pavements, or in the play of light and shadow cast by some street-lamp upon puddles at the corner of a shabby street, traces of the beautiful, degraded, dishonoured, suffering, sorrowful, but still the *deus absconditus*. It was a search for the lost lineaments of the most high in the most low; hence the strange sense of dedication, of quest, in which we walked; anywhere, everywhere, we might receive a sign, that hidden and degraded god might sign to us, reproachful, sorrowful, majestic as the face imprinted upon the Holy Shroud.

On the wall of the Jennings' room in Blackheath, successor to that first Cambridge room, scene of so many marvellous, but unrecorded, monologues, hung a painting by Magritte (I saw it again, after many years, in the Magritte exhibition at the Tate Gallery, in 1972). In the foreground a cannon, emblem of coming war or revolution, was pointed towards a wall or flimsy screen, partitioned into sections. I ought to remember them all, for Heaven knows I gazed at that picture often enough. These were the fragments of a world, not, like Eliot's, 'shored against our ruins', but to be demolished when the cannon fired. There was a section of the façade of a house; a woman's torso; the trunks of some trees; a patch of blue sky with white clouds. Several others escape me—it would be easy to check, but let it serve as an instance of memory's unreliability, its blanks and its blind spots. For all our intoxicating sense of undisclosed marvels under the thin surface of consciousness, we yet saw in that gun pointed at the flimsy fabric of a painted scene the true emblem of the future of our world. It did not dismay us; that is how the spirit of Revolution wanted it to be; the cannon, now about to fire, was our will.

Emptied of this *mana* it is hard to understand, in retrospect, how the lumber of Surrealism once invested a passing host of gods; but the Host was real enough, as the approaching war was presently to show. The strange spirits which were let loose upon our world made their entrance through 'possession' such as ours. Its English form seemed harmless enough; philanthropic, as Charles and his Marxist friends conceived it; yet our possession was akin not only to French *Surréalisme* but to the more violent upsurge of the irrational forces in Nazi Germany. None of those Surrealists or Mass Observers at that time engaged in opening the dungeons of the unconscious and freeing energies imprisoned there had the wisdom to gauge, or the power to control or to transmute what came to light.

Charles had the gift of seeing as pictures in a diviner's crystal glass events forming in that medium (whatever it may be) from which material effects appear to flow from anterior mental causes. Humphrey recognized the signs everywhere, took marvellous photographs of those significant images that seemed to speak to us, as do dream-symbols, from within. But I in that dream was a mere somnambulist, passively possessed though not inspired. As we enjoy our dreams, even our worst nightmares, so fraught are they with that knowledge which is our own being, so I in a sense enjoyed this strange condition, with its intoxicating sense of being in the power of a life beyond my small humanity and, above all, beyond good and evil. 'Ye shall be as gods . . .'; and so we felt ourselves at that time to be.

85

The Cambridge word 'detachment' we no longer used: now we were 'observers', God's spies seeing far beneath us the human scene, as if we were ourselves at once spectators and authors of that play but not its enactors.

Just before the outbreak of the second world war, the unreality upon which we were treading rose like a mounting tidal wave; we seemed, straws and corks and drifting fragments that we were, to be soaring to the crest of some strange realization (for we were, God knows, upon a quest, in our *voyage au bout de la nuit*) when the wave broke and crashed us all down. For Charles, I was the wave that broke; for myself, I seemed no more able to alter or stop my course than a breaking wave. I was in the power of unconscious forces stronger than I knew, as I so passively drifted on a dream.

Two terrible images which were certainly not reflected from Charles's dream or the dreams of the mass-mind, haunted me at that time. Launcelot, riding in quest of the Holy Grail, entering a room in a certain castle, sees upon a table, covered with a white cloth, what he believes to be the Grail; but when he lifts the cloth he finds beneath it the body of a dead babe. From the same Arthurian mythology came the other symbol—the knight who watches in the Chapel Perilous before a sanctuary lamp, sees at midnight a black hand come and extinguish the light. I have no words for the dread with which these two symbolic images filled me; nor have I, even now, attempted to analyse the complex of guilt and sorrow, remorse and dread, the life behind those masks. The *objets trouvés* I had hoped to find were not these.

One of those drawn into the net of Mass-Observation was an astrologer, Gay Taylor; and I must truthfully admit that her astrology and other esoteric studies interested me a great deal more than the sociology of leftist idealism which seemed to me (as Blake says of politics) 'something other than human life'. It was doubltless my own despair which made me turn to such things, seeking an escape; but I was surely not alone in my time in my growing inability to continue to live by the values of a materialist philosophy.

Even in its most magical and most idealistic form, as Charles embodied it, I found it increasingly claustrophobic, unendurable.

Of all the friends of a lifetime, as in retrospect I understand, Gay was one of the most remarkable, as well as one of the most loved. She understood me better than I did myself; sustained me in times of deepest spiritual danger, never condemned or relinquished me; and besides all that, she was fun to know; she touched in me the springs of laughter, of the life-enhancing absurdity of the near at hand. Under the influence of draught cider (she called it 'the truth drug') what all-embracing conversations did we not have. Yet, like those 'messengers' from Kafka's Castle, her outward aspect gave no clue to her essence. She was among the many 'dotty' correspondents who answered Charles's advertisement for Mass Observers in the New Statesman. She volunteered to address envelopes, and came to Blackheath; and although Charles disliked her (perhaps because he sensed in her one of those woman allies of other women who are so dangerous to marriages) remained a Mass Observer long after the movement had ceased to be more than an agency for market research. But market research satisfied something in Gay's nature; she treasured those chance encounters with ordinary, anonymous, and—to use a word she herself often used (verbally underlined) 'odd' members of the human race. ('Peculiar' was another of her underlined words; of possible explanations of any event she preferred always the paranormal.)

Charles observed these odd beings as specimens made remote by the telescope of his 'observation'. Tom Harrisson regarded them as subjects of 'anthropological' interest ('loving' them but as most anthropologists love their primitive tribes, or animal behaviourists their apes). To Gay these were human souls, 'odd' and 'peculiar' as she was herself, but, like her, lost travellers in this most peculiar world. Like some Russian holy beggar she saw her life of odd encounters as fulfilling some unknown but Heaven-directed purpose; because she was a stranger people would talk to

87

her of their troubles, tell her, perhaps, stories long pent up in silence. As a born (if unsuccessful) novelist, these stories satisfied her insatiable curiosity about life and people. But she also prayed for those who asked for her prayers; and when, on her death, I inherited her papers, I found scores of cards, made out in her neat, microscopic hand (reminiscent of Emily Brontë's) filled in with the same meticulous care as the astonishingly accurate horoscopes she used to cast, with the names of people she was praying for during any month: names, reasons for prayer (sickness or some other trouble) and any other relevant matter. Some of these were friends but most were strangers she had met on her travels, or perhaps relatives of these whom she had never seen. On the card by her death-bed, my name was among the rest; and my daughter's.

She kept, besides, a note-book in which she recorded her daily periods of prayer; the time, the depth of concentration, the distractions, or illuminations, or other things to be noted in this, the work of her life. This record took the form of charts, not diary notes. 'Keep your life hidden' was her rule; a phrase taken (was it?) from Lao Tze or some other Chinese sage of the Tao. Only in secret, in hidden lives, she held, is perfect freedom possible, uncorrupted by ambition, undistracted, undismayed by the judgement of others. She aimed at perfect truthfulness, though, God knows, in no sanctimonious way. Indeed when I first knew her perfect truthfulness was perfect truthfulness about sex and her relationships with men; which shocked my ingrained puritanism, even at that time. But it was the same truthfulness that she later brought to her equally difficult relationship with God.

That was long after. At the time I first met Gay her life was as totally catastrophic as my own was fast becoming. She had already published a novel in which she told the story—as it then seemed to her—of her marriage triangle with Hal Taylor (founder of the Golden Cockerel press, which in the early 'twenties was publishing beautiful hand-printed books) and one of the authors they published, a well-known short-story writer of the time. Her husband had died, leaving his money to relations; and Gay, penniless, soon found herself deserted by her shabby lover. With truly feminine illogic she blamed her husband with unforgiving bitterness, finding every excuse for the lover, and angrily protesting that she had been betrayed by both. Maybe, in the light of inner truth, she was right; or maybe she protested too much. At one time she read every document relating to Mary, Queen of Scots; she was herself a Stuart, but she may have had deeper reasons for seeking to understand the inwardness of Mary's dark and devious marriage entanglements.

Whatever standards of judgement she may have applied they were certainly not those of conventional—or any other—morality, but of a more vital truth. The intangible ambience of her culture was, I think, that of the Powyses, whom she had known; some of their books, also, I have inherited from her. In *Wolf Solent* (annotated in that neat hand, with all the place-names carefully identified) I reentered, years later, what I recognized, with a pang of nostalgia, as Gay's world. The same half-mystical, half-erotic love of the landscape of the south-west of England— Glastonbury, Gloucester, the Cotswolds—and of certain buildings. Like Thomas Hardy, whose poetry she supremely loved, her father had been a rural architect and restorer of churches. I inherited, too, a great collection of postcards of rustic churches, pagan foliate faces or lewd rustic forms peeping from roof-boss or capital. Not only the interest or the beauty, but, Powys-like, the 'feel', the secret life of places was her secret delight.

Gay's pursuit of 'truth', of reality—of, as it proved, 'God'— was as totally uncommitted to morality as that of John Cowper Powys's Wolf Solent: like Powys's characters she tested every experience, every person on the delicate, subtly responsive, fastidious, but also erotic nerve-endings of her own life. Yet in her appearance she was like a caricature of a lady novelist of the 'twenties with her brow curtained by her long fine fringe, her dangling earrings, her cigarette-holder, her verbal underlinings. Like Dickens's Miss Faversham, she remained as she had been at the time of her great drama; she had enough to do, for the rest of her life, to discover the truth about that one experience. Like many women who live alone she talked non-stop when she was not, with oddities and affectations that were the hardened residue, perhaps, of her once kittenish charm (she adored all cats, and had a series of her own, all people) 'back in the 'twenties', as she often used to say. But even when she was not being witty, the penny-plain world became, in her company, 'twopence coloured'.

In those Blackheath days she pitied my plight and was anxious to extend to me her friendship as to a younger unfortunate, interesting, misunderstood, desperate woman. And God knows every woman needs a woman friend with whom she can be truthful; as it is impossible to be quite truthful or quite at ease, altogether quite naturally oneself, with the opposite sex, in any relationship, however intimate. So it befell at a time when she no more than I had any thought that the journey of life might prove to be a pilgrimage, we became, unawares, what to the end we remained, fellow pilgrims. For we were both on a journey, though at the time with no sense of destination. We were neither of us looking for God, but, much rather, doing our utmost to get away from him. Gay, finer in her responses than I, far less hypocritical, less heavy-handed both in her morality and her immorality, was nevertheless inwardly one of 'God's fools'. She was a mystic; in later years receiving several experiences described in the classics of mystical literature, including the 'sun-flower' (as she called it) of the heart. Of these she felt herself to be so profoundly unworthy that she struggled for years to avoid them. Yet for years I treated her in a most off-hand manner, rather ashamed of her than otherwise among my less eccentric friends.

But once I remember—years later, long after the war—catching, from a bus in the King's Road, a glimpse of Gay, her scarf (as much a part of her habit as a nun's wimple) tied round her head, above the familiar 'fringe', coming from an ironmonger's shop carrying a tin of paraffin for the smelly stove she used for economy. She was very poor indeed, for she refused to take any job more regular than her occasional market-research, because this would have interrupted her thoughts and her meditation; and indeed her incorrigible sloth, as she called it. When she published her second book she took the pseudonym 'Loren Hurnscot', anagram on her two besetting sins, sloth and rancour, so she said.

I doubt if her refusal to do what is ordinarily called work was really sloth, though rancour against the husband who left her penniless may have had some part in it. But in the living of her inner life no one was less slothful; and to Gay the living of that inner life was the important thing, the whole meaning of her existence. 'You see', she once exclaimed to me (it was just by the letter-box at the corner of Paulton's Square and Danvers Street) 'all I *have* is my life.' Again in retrospect I discern an echo of Wolf Solent; or was Gay, rather, among those 'period' people whose way of being, of experiencing, of living a life, gave Powys the matter of his art?

So it was when I caught, as it were, an objective glimpse of her, at a moment when she did not know she was observed, when between us there was no relationship or contact. Carrying the fuel of the poor in her small refined hands, I saw my friend as she was, 'in God's eye', so to say.

Since her death I have been reading the books she left me; Berdaiev and Boehme and Julian of Norwich. I gave away my own Hardy and kept hers, every page lived over, every place identified, every person. The message I had from her through a medium—if she it was—was characteristic of an astrologer who had six planets in air: 'I have adjusted', she said, 'almost *too* (underlined) easily!' Was it really Gay? She herself would certainly have wished me to believe the unearthly explanation.

It seems inevitable that for a materialist society political ideologies should supplant religion. My father's politics, like Plato's, like AE's, was conceived as an attempt to make 'the politics of time' conform with 'the politics of eternity', to build the Holy City 'on earth as it is in Heaven'. But what was the holy city of the Marxists and what its laws? To me then, as now, the responsibilities of life seemed personal issues; conscience the arbiter of our acts and aspirations, whether towards ourselves or towards others. It may be said that my life presents a desperately unconvincing argument for that way of life, and that if I had conformed to some rule (Catholic or Marxist) and recognized that what I have called conscience has been mere wilfulness, my daimon a will o' the wisp, I might have done, at least, less harm. But that the assumption of any ideology should replace the perennial task and quest of the soul—should take from us the possibility of damnation or beatitude no social order can confer or take away—is, to me, still unimaginable.

The poetic side of Mass-Observation captivated me; but the political side made me shrink and shudder. There was something in the faces, in the spiritual atmosphere, of some of Charles's Communist friends which I sensed as evil. I remember once some Chinese visited him, whose like I had never imagined to exist, so terrible they were; Marxism had its own style. And yet at that time the Good was identified, in the minds of our generation, with Leftism. Not to be a Marxist then was held to be a mark either of incorrigible selfishness or lack of seriousness. I felt, no less than the Marxists among us, that the current of history which flows in one direction only, flowed the way that they were going; and much of the sense of god-like, invincible power that then possessed us came from this sense of flowing with the tide. To move with that tide seemed even to be a kind of virtue in itself, an implicit faith in the purpose of whatever hidden power conducts the world, even though that power was at the same time denied mind or purpose. Many of us who would not use the word God nevertheless lived by faith in the life-force itself, and to that life-force abandoned ourselves.

And yet I could not go with that mainstream of evolution, if such it was. But of one thing only I was sure, in rejecting

Marxism: that I was putting myself upon the losing side.

So to live in Charles's dream, noble though that dream was, I could not have continued: sooner or later the break must have come between two poets each with a daimon to obey. Never was I unhappy through any fault of Charles's, never were my tears caused by him; they came from deeper and more hidden springs than domestic quarrels. That I hurt a man so fine by marrying him for inadequate, indeed for deeply neurotic, reasons, lies heavily on my conscience; but to have remained with him, I being who I was and am, would have been to injure him, so I believe, even more. I did not mean to betray Charles; but those who do not know themselves, who are alienated from themselves, cannot help betraying whether they go or stay. I seemed to love him— thought I loved him, though our love was rather a poetic fantasia than a marriage.

But had I no sense of the responsibilities I had incurred by marriage to Charles, by our children? I had not. As between those duties (which many will say were plainly now those which ought to have come before all else) and the duties which I inwardly still knew I had betrayed before all this tangle began, there was never, for me, any question.

Those who keep those rules of society made to protect human life from unendurable extremes neither inflict nor endure such miseries as I both caused and suffered. By social standards their morality is wise and right, mine insane and indefensible. But, by that morality, was Charles ever my husband? Neither of us, I think, believed in our relationship, whose very essence had been its freedom, from the day it became a marriage; that was not what either of us had meant.

CHAPTER FIVE

The Demon Eros

I LEFT Charles Madge because I fell in love, if Eros be love. I left with no more conflict of conscience than a bird whose wings have been clipped and who one day finds that the pinnae have grown again; or a fish frozen in the ice that finds a river flowing and consciousness restored. Who can withstand the flow of returning life? Those may well condemn me who understand love as *caritas*; but there is only one judge to whose condemnation I must assent, the Judge at the heart of life; a confronation more terrible than with any moral code, but of a different order. If in that Judgement I stand condemned it is more likely to be for heartlessness than for falling in love.

Charles was I think in Bolton with Tom Harisson, and I was alone; free and alone for the first time since, perhaps, my Cambridge student days. Is there any young woman who does not, when thus for the first time alone, straighten like a sapling long tied down, to the form she had, or should have had? I was invited for a week-end by a friend who had a country cottage; and another guest, whom I had never met, was driving down in his car, and would take me. I had heard his name (he had been a Cambridge contemporary) and that he was astonishingly handsome and something of a Don Juan. He was in fact very shy, and we scarcely found a word to say to one another as we drove first out of London, then into country roads, and at last, leaving the car at the end of a lane, set out to find our host's cottage, hidden in beech-woods which overshadowed us with an older, sweeter world than any I had seen for long. As we walked deeper and deeper into these woods I began to remember; how long how long since I had been in this world of nature which had once been mine! My sophisticated companion too seemed to lose, step by step, his man-of-the-world guise, and trod softly as a deer among the trees. We reached at last the cottage, the archetypal cottage of all fairy-tales, overhung with honeysuckle and sweet roses. There was a huge log-fire in a great chimney where we sat, after our evening meal, drowsed in wood-smoke and the tangible silence of the woods. Our host had filled jugs with great bunches of wild flowers, and we drank water drawn up from an old well.

Next day we rode in the woods along bridle-paths; my fellow-guest, as we walked back after leaving our horses, lifted a long straight pine-pole and threw it; he had 'tossed the caber', ancient ancestral skill. His handsome features, his dark hair, white skin and blue eyes, his light tread and his low musical voice suddenty took on a meaning which was not merely that of 'a handsome man'; he was no longer an alien but of my own country, the country lost before all my sorrows began, lost before I began. Yet I had at this time so far forgotten who I was, and everything once dear to me, that his name (a combination of two of those few Highland names which recur in the songs and the history of Scotland) had not even made me think of him as a Scot; I had thought of him as a former student of one of the Cambridge colleges and an acquaintance of this and that Cambridge con-temporary; but in that moment the image changed, and I remembered who I was and saw what he was, as in a sudden anamnesis I ceased to be a somnambulist. As he stood among the great beeches he seemed like a messenger; from my childhood, from Bavington, from over the Border; from my ancestors. I felt that they from their long buried dust awoke in the sudden passionate love which the bearer of a name so often loved by them had evoked in me. In falling in love with this Alastair, as at that moment I did, it was not himself alone, or principally, whom I saw and loved, but all those ancestors, and all the echoes and resonances of their lost world and my lost world, and my lost self and perhaps his lost self. To me he was the bearer of the race and its living dust, of the pentatonic and hexatonic melodies of Scotland; he was the bright distant mountains of the imagination, the golden country. The spirits of my mother and my grandmother clamoured in me like ghosts then for the life-blood they had been denied.

My grandmother had ended her life, a very old woman, in a house in a grim industrial town where my widowed Aunt Jean lived on after the death of the husband who had brought her there, among sooty brick streets of back-to-back houses. In a dark and cheerless kitchen the old woman had sat in her dignified old-fashioned black dress with its braided bust and white lace at the neck, her voluminous serge skirt covering her feet, a white Shetland shawl about her shoulders, and a lace cap on her white hair. There she sat remembering things far away and beyond recall. Over the kitchen range hung an oil-painting, brown with age and varnish, of a highland river in spate pouring over its stones; and for her that picture was the gate out of the drab world where she sat a helpless prisoner of bricks and mortar. She told me, so I remember, that often she would look so long at that painted burn that at last it would seem to her real water flowing over real stones, and she there. This Alastair, on that very morning, brought with overwhelming vividness my dead grandmother to mind; I could smell, strongly and unmistakably, her peculiar clean fresh human scent, wafted back from childhood.

It had been Charles's grandmother who had, in a series of terrifying dreams, warned him and raged at him for his union with me, in the very first weeks of it, visiting him night after night and leaving him prostrate. He did not heed her, and still less did I; it seems to me now incredible that we should have dared to go against monitions so unmistakable, whether from the world of spirits in a literal or only in a figurative sense. She had of course been right—that world always is; regarded ancestrally, Charles and I should never have been united. We had defied the ancestors when we entered upon a relationship which they did not sanction.

I conceived, there and then for that incarnation of an ancestral image, a deep and long-enduring passion, for which I would have undergone every traditional ordeal with joy; the symbol of that passion was for me the story of the Black Bull of Norroway, and I the girl who followed her lover to the world's end. It was now my turn to say over the words of the archetypal story. 'The iron shoes I wore for thee, the mountain of ice I clamb for thee, the bluidy sark I wrang for thee, and wilt thou no wauken and turn to me?' Yet in this passion there was nothing personal at all; it was as if the ancestors cried out in my blood that race is all, the individual only a bright ripple upon the ever-flowing river. Swept on like a flake of snow upon the surface of that river (to use an image from the ancestral poetry) we are, for the time, the consciousness of the river itself; and so I felt myself, in this atavistic and ardent passion, to be. All we then experience has the beauty and profound meaning of a unity and a wholeness, nothing is deformed, broken and fragmentary (as we ourselves are) but all brought to a perfection which is the creation of countless generations. In this collective experience primitive people must surely participate, in a vital current unknown to dispossessed modern man; even perhaps animals—who knows how deep are the currents of life? What else, in the deepest sense, is carnal desire but the will of the ancestors?

At the same moment that I fell passionately in love, I believed in—remembered rather—the divine world. To say 'in God' would be too theological a word for that insight into the sacramental essence of life. My eyes seemed now to behold the earth and sky for the first time, although it was not in fact for the first time, but a re-awakening after a long death or sleep of something I had once and for ever known, and had long forgotten. Not all my intellectual studies had opened to me the nature of things as did this passionate physical love; and I can only testify to my own experience of the paradox through which the lowest (if physical passion be such) was for me at that time a revelation of the highest. My renewed vision of the holy was in the depths of carnal desire.

I could not have guessed the immense power of the race, had I not experienced it. I had not, after all, any great individual affection for my Scottish ancestors, who now threw my individual identity (which I had so long struggled to preserve) to the winds. I have since seen again that archaic world where the identity of men or women is that of family, scarcely at all of themselves as individuals; this or that Hector or John-Donald or Jessie or Annie, is 'a Macleod' or 'a MacKinnon' or a Campbell or a MacIsaac, and therein lies their sense of identity and dignity; each raised to the stature of a family whose memories and deeds, fading almost imperceptibly from human memory into history, history into legend, is inseparable and indistinguishable from the story of their own lives, whose events are scarcely distinct, in their own minds, from the stories of their forefathers; at best they can add something memorable to the record. The glens and the isles where those same ancestors have lived, and where they live in turn, are their country not by deed of property but by the renewal, again and again, of the covenant of life. In this respect the poorest crofters of the Western Isles are like members of some noble family, Palaeologi or Howards or Percys, and often of purer blood than these. Their culture too is racial and ancestral; theirs by right of birth, along with their language and their skills; like the skills of their dogs, a race like themselves repeating and transmitting a pure strain, a collective pattern. It is to this racial being, not to anything individual in us, that erotic passion surely belongs, sweeping away all that to friendship matters most, all the shared interests and values of the world we consciously inhabit.

I chanced (long afterwards) to be on one of those isles when an old woman died; poor, almost illiterate, her horizon bounded in the south by Ardnamurchan, in the north by Kyle, and in the west, on a clear day, by South Uist; her pride that she was of the Clanranald. In the small square grave-yard, tangled with bramble and escalonia and overgrown with rank grass and nettles, a hole was dug for her among the bones of former generations; bones of old women and men scarcely yet forgotten were turned up to make a place for her among them. A piece of pasture-land adjoining had been given by the Laird, so dense was the population of the dead in that rank square; but the people would not use it, they would rather return to the hallowed earth of the dead from whose collective and immortal life they had themselves briefly emerged, to be laid back in the ancestral loam with the rites of Catholic burial. There are many such grave-yards in the Isles, scandalous by English notions, but that is how members of an ancient race wish to be buried, in the earth of their own people. My love for Alastair was like their desire to be dug back into ancestral clay.

Conscience never spoke to me one word to suggest it my duty to remain with Charles; 'caught in that sensual music' I was deaf, it may be, to spirits from higher regions who could have taught me another wisdom than that of the flesh, and another love. Perhaps I was, and still am, deeply mistaken, blind to some farther truth which, had I seen it, would have made me stay. Even if that be so, I still would plead that I could not have reached that farther truth without this epiphany of natural love; could not, by remaining a som-nambulist in his house, have helped either Charles or myself. I had in Ilford seen too many of the dead living quietly and unobtrusively and respectably, fearing above all else the voices of life which could but disrupt and throw into ruin the false constructions so many build to shelter them from the terrible energies of life. This I could not do, nor force upon Charles a partnership of such a kind. I loved Charles, in one sense, too much to stay with him; in another, not enough. My sense of what was honourable—for I really did think I was acting as in honour bound—must seem strange. I see now that it is possible that I was deceiving myself; I wanted to be free and therefore persuaded myself that this was also the right course. I argued with myself that what is wrong for one must be wrong for the other; that the children of two people mis-allied would also suffer from the contin-uance of a falsehood. I do not think that for leaving Charles the Judge will condemn me, for I acted in obedience to the most profound truth I at that time knew. For having married him—for that I may indeed stand condemned. The consequences of such a deep untruth must always be, one way or another terrible.

I had promised, it may be said; but—apart from the fact that, as a Marxist, Charles himself had believed no more than I in the sacramental and binding nature of the marriage contract we had made—the I who had promised had promised in my absence; and this must often be so, even in many formally Christian marriages made in good faith. People do not necessarily know who or what they are, may be dead or asleep at the time a promise is given. And what if the sleeper wake? Those who do not know themselves, the somnambulists, are sure, sooner or later, to betray. A voice did then speak to me, daimon or guardian angel, or ancestral wisdom but not in the name of social duty. It seemed to me then that I was shown the falsehood of years of wandering from the world of living reality; a veil was withdrawn, and behind the outer I saw the inner aspect of my life, and all my edifice crumbled. But does not love consist in mutual tolerance and patience, a compassion for the weaknesses and human limitations of another person, the sharing of the daily tasks of life in kindness? I know, I know; but then I did not know. Besides, all these may be given not in love but in a kind of remorse for not loving. Is not love, upon all planes, a divine energy, a transforming passion, a mystery? It comes not from conscious will but from unconscious depths. Love cannot be domesticated; though, when it is present, perhaps it may enable two people to get somehow through the Heaven knows hard enough ordeal of life. Yet when love is reasonable, is it not because the flames are out?

Is not Eros then more demon than daemon? The story of Phaedra, tortured and driven both to crime and to death excites only pity and horror. Yet her situation is a reality, one of the current predicaments of women struggling in the toils of life. Plato in the Phaedrus more light-heartedly lists the anti-social sins of Eros; but he too ends by saying,

100

Heaven forgive those who raise merely social objections against a god, a divine energy.

From the day I left Charles I have never again lived with lover or husband, but carried my burden alone, assumed the consequences of my own acts. With the courage only of my egoism, it may be; but whatever the motive, I have not, from the time of that re-awakening, allowed others to rescue me. I had to get away from the false constructions of years; perhaps I had to release Charles also, whom I had so undeservedly involved in my desperate flight. It may be that I made, into erotic love, a descent, a fall; but even so, I was so strongly summoned to my own place that, up or down, there I had to go.

As for that Alastair, I see now that he was the occasion, not the cause. Even then I never thought of consulting him, for my decision to leave Charles was, it seemed to me, no affair of his. If some part of me wildly longed to be united with his divine beauty, another part knew perfectly well that my passion had nothing to do with such things as marriage and cohabitation. We had absolutely nothing, humanly speaking, in common, upon which we could have built a life. He himself certainly never contemplated any such thing, for he was, I think, cautious and conventional. He probably thought I was making great a mistake in leaving my husband; 'Such a beautiful sensitive face to go through the world alone,' I remember his saying (indicating, in this phrase, with a remote echo of West Highland tact, that I could look for no support from him). I did not, at this, feel, as might be imagined, self-pity because my lover did not want me; rather I felt something like surprised annoyance that this man should see me as one more attractive conquest of Don Juan (for whom all women are merely variations of Woman) whereas I knew myself a poet, following, however tortuously, a destiny to which Don Juan might himself prove to be the sacrifice. 'The dice are loaded too heavily against you,' he said, when I told him that I intended to make my life as a writer; but destiny is not a cast of the dice (*'Un coup de dés jamais n'abolira l'hazard,'* we had

101

liked to quote) nor does vocation calculate its chances. I felt at last that I was upon my own path again, and that was enough.

What Alastair was like, as a person, I neither knew nor cared. I was not interested in him; a fact which does me no credit. I never noticed what kind of human personality he had; to have done so would have dimmed and obscured the image of the god he for me embodied. It did not then occur to me that this was unkind or unjust, for the miracle of his beauty seemed of far greater value than any merely human attributes he might possess. For his immortal soul I did not care, only for his mortal beauty. Insofar as he departed from 'the beautiful itself' which in him I saw reflected, I would have liked to take a sculptor's mallet and rectify the form. When he was actually present (fortunately that was seldom) I was always strangely put out as if by a double image; for never did the temporal and the eternal quite coincide. It was when he was not there that I most adored his beauty, in the contemplation of his recollected features, rectified by the archetype.

I was led unawares into a kind of asceticism, so far can passionate desire, even in its lowest mode, over-reach any natural mark. But sexual desire is an incandescent state in which we look deep into certain aspects of being. These insights are the fruits of an almost unendurable intensity of passion, a sacrificial immolation of mere carnality. The whole structure of nature which as a child I had innocently lived, as a student intellectually contemplated, now revealed itself to me burning with an interior light and glory, awe-inspiring. This state, known to all lovers, glorifies every blade of grass with a sacramental quality of holiness. Though I longed for the participation of this vision (which is, to the imagination of love, the supreme joy) my lover's actual presence merely dimmed and obliterated this epiphany of creation itself.

In retrospect I wonder if it is not the reflections upon love in the lover's absence that count for most. Gay, in comic vein, used to say that she used to send her lovers away so

102

that she could really *think* about them; an activity the lover's actual presence merely interrupted. Nor did she mean erotic fantasy, but, rather, contemplation, pondering over, the nature and meaning of love. And I wonder if long conversations with Gay on the theme of love were not, in the last instance, far more rewarding than mere 'love'. What was love but the mere *prima materia* of those reflections, ponderings, and indeed occasionally, poems? If I could choose, in Paradise, between the beloved's arms and conversation and cider with Gay, I should not hesitate to choose the Platonic dialogue, and the cider.

I must have divined intuitively that in the sexual mystery the creator is (as the Dance of Shiva expresses and signifies) also the destroyer; for I remember a dream of that time so vivid that I can breathe again its atmosphere as I write. In the meadow opposite West View (restored, in that dream, to its long-lost aspect as in my childhood before its trees were felled and shops were built) I saw Alastair ploughing, walking round the four sides of the sunlit flowering field. My two children were running after him, happily, as it seemed. But the voice which in dreams can speak so clearly and unequivocally then pronounced the words, 'Death, the reaper'; and I recognized in the guise of my lover the figure who on the twenty-first Tarot card wields the scythe, trampling men and women down into the earth, from which hands and crowned heads are seen sprouting only to be lopped off and dug back into the mire. So much for the ancestors and their acre; so much for the process of generation and death. What sex sows, death reaps.

> Whate'er is born of mortal birth
> Must be consumed with the earth.
> To rise from generation free . . .

It seemed to me then that it was the god of the life-force who had me in his power; but I wonder if after all it was not the poetic daimon who used the lesser deity? I began at last to write poems, a few grains of gold calcined from all that dross of life in the fires of an overwhelming physical passion.

103

So much anguish for grains of gold so minute! But the daimons do not measure such things by our standards, for their object is to produce the gold and they heap on the fuel until the transmutation is brought about, regardless of suffering. I had never suffered so acutely as at this time when, having left Charles, I waited in vain for word or sign from my demon lover; yet I knew I would rather thus suffer than return to the painless state in which I had formerly been; for now, after long years, I was alive. I endured the endless hours from cup of tea to cigarette, each day a slow ordeal whose end I could not envisage, but which I knew I must undergo. 'It is a terrible thing to fall into the hands of the living God'; for sexual passion is the operation of the living God upon the lowest plane, as it may be, of existence. Yet in that existence, one level cannot be separated from another, and only upon that ground upon which we really stand will we experience the impact of a reality confined to none. If I stood in a low place on the scale of perfection, at that low place at which I then really was I must enter upon the long painful transmutation of love. Sexual love was the best of which I was then capable; it was a reality; it was, for me, at that time, reality itself. I had for too long known what it is to be divorced from reality to doubt or question that light which now shone in my darkness.

Every moment is the consequence of every preceding moment, the sum to which our life, at that moment, adds up; therefore we are grounded in the whole cosmos. In this whole each moment is our location, our standing-place, it is what we have made and what has made us, and therefore is what we are, the only ground upon which we can build; therefore it is exactly what it should be and must be, and exactly appropriate to our condition. In this sense it may well be that a condition of suffering is the best condition in which we can be, the only state of which we are capable; and the most dynamic, the most potent source of transformation and transmutation. I think I drew strength, at this time and for years to come, from my knowledge, for the first time since Bavington, that I was where I should be, that I had come into my own; painful to the extreme limit of endurance as that place and state might be.

Certainly at the outset I had no intention of undergoing suffering of any kind; on the contrary, I wildly dreamed of earthly love; dreamed rather than hoped. A migrant bird sets off to fly across the ocean without the intention of enduring storms; but the impulse to fly is so strong that no storm will turn its flight. I no more calculated than the bird; yet I believe that if I had known in advance all I would have to undergo in poverty, isolation, and the toils of unrequited passion, nothing would have deterred me. Being what I was, I had to go my way; so it is when we begin to live by the energies of life itself. The immense strength of desire seemed to give me a power of achieving and enduring anything and everything. I seemed to myself, then, to be inexhaustible, unconquerable. To poverty and the lonely confrontation with the world I had formerly so feared I now gave no more thought than water fears a waterfall or a meteorite empty space. I suffered, indeed, with unremitting intensity; and yet, like the souls in Purgatory, I threw myself into the flames with joy. Doubtless I had to suffer so intensely because I had so much from which I must be purged; yet even at the lowest level, the pain and the joy of Purgatory are inseparable; and I knew myself to be, now, at last, no longer in Hades but in the holy world of life.

The daimons may have known what they were about; but if I was in their power I was not in their confidence. Yet I obeyed them, after a fashion; collaborated, to some extent; wrote the poems they wrung from me as best I could. It must for them have been like breaking a wild colt, always trying to bolt for freedom; yet in part I was on their side against myself; reluctantly and in tears and anguish I did what they wanted me to do. I did not spare myself, and they did not spare me. I never looked back, even though it was in part illusion, the will o' the wisp of carnal love, that led me on.

Among the threads woven into the pattern, one may have

105

been a curse from whose consequences I could not have hoped to escape. At the cottage in the woods where I fell under the power, for good or evil or both, of the spell of Alastair, I afterwards discovered that my first husband had stayed, after I left him, and when it had belonged to a former owner. Had he called up, then, in his grief and rage, powers in which he doubtless would not have believed, and of which I too was at that time ignorant? I had thought when I left him that I could escape scot-free; but the forces of nature operate whether or not we believe in them or know their laws. If we roll a stone down a slope it will take its course whether we push it deliberately or inadvertently; so, unawares, we may activate daimonic powers, stumbling blindly among them as among rocks on the edge of a precipice. So I believe I fell under a spell worked unwittingly (though not without the will or wish to injure me in revenge for the injury I had done him), when I walked unawares into that deceptively enchanting and enchanted cottage among the old nature-magic of ancient woods. Cause and effect operate on many planes; and there was a pattern in this fatality of which one strand may well have been my first husband's cry for revenge.

Yet the laws of such causes and operations may themselves be subject to other laws. A disaster may by a curse be loosed upon us like an avalanche or a storm at sea; but disaster itself be a means of blessing and turned to good. In any case, whether I was cursed by ill-will or blessed by angels, the suffering would have been the same. Had I been innocent I would have been invulnerable to the curse, or the blessing less painful; in either case I reaped what I had sown, experienced what was my due.

War came, that breaker-up of lives, and Alastair (true to his name and race) immediately enlisted and was soon posted abroad. So that I was providentially saved—and he too—from what might have become a sordid entanglement. I see in retrospect that interruption of an incipient love affair which at the time seemed a most cruel thwarting, as a powerful intervention of the guardian daimons (who make use alike of all conditions of peace or of war) whose protection I at that time scarcely deserved. They made themselves very clear; their purposes were not at one with my carnal desires. I remember still with a kind of pity for the longings and dreams, however vain, however blind, the perfect beauty of an early summer day and myself in the very heart of that summer waiting for my lover, who had promised to come for his last leave before he was sent abroad. On that day I walked not on knives but upon air. The light was of a radiance not of this common earth. Fringing the swift waters of the little beck flowing through my meadow in a dale in Cumberland were marigold and mimulus and anemone and water-avons, and, as I vividly remember, a patch of speedwell of brightest blue. These I remember because they seemed to promise a lover's swift arrival. My white house was swept and garnished and I awaited his coming as that inexpressible and perfect felicity for which all long. The time had almost come; when instead a boy with a telegram: 'All leave cancelled.' I went on blankly looking at the speedwell flowers.

I am glad now that he never came; that no mortal lover entered that valley where for the next years I lived with my children. Indeed for all the time I remained there it was as if guarded by a circle of magic force, a place of refuge, of vision, of poetry, and, the anguish of my unpurged passion notwithstanding, of beatitude.

Even now I find it almost incredible that a life can undergo so many mutations; my one life has been like a series of lives whose stories are like so many reincarnations. I now see that each of these transformations of outer circumstances corresponds to some inner state. It is naïve indeed to suppose ourselves the victims of circumstances, who are continually weaving and fashioning according to our dreams the texture of the solid-seeming world, which reflects back to us what in imagination we generate. Sometimes the plasticity of the world to our states of consciousness seems indeed astonishing. So, my awakening from somnambulism into a natural passion of great purity and intensity, revived

107

the memory of my ancestral roots; and my longing to return to these was almost immediately followed by a period in which I lived in a place in many ways akin to Bavington, yet echoed and repeated on a higher octave, as it were, more luminous, more complex. The natural world was thrown open to me again, and I was permitted to return, for a season, to Paradise. Yet all this came about without any volition of my own; I was led, blindfold, as if by some angelic minister of grace.

CHAPTER SIX

Rescue

TO SAY that this change was the work of my daimon is not to show ingratitude to the friends who were its agents; on the contrary, it is to say that Janet (Adam Smith) and Michael Roberts were to me friends literally Heaven-sent. For what other reason could they have invited me to go with them to Penrith, where the Newcastle Royal Grammar School (on whose staff Michael then was) had been evacuated? Janet and Michael saved me, body and soul, at that time. I had thought of Michael rather as Charles's friend than as mine; for he had included some of Charles's poems in his *New Country* and *Faber Book of Modern Verse,* and befriended him in the days when his attic flat in Fitzroy Square had been a rendezvous for young poets. Janet, as literary editor of *The Listener,* had published the first few poems of mine to appear outside Cambridge but Michael had included none in the Faber book; rightly, for none were good enough, and such qualities as they had potentially were not those of that time, or of the movement whose spokesman he had made himself. For Michael it was who, a few years older than Auden, Spender, Charles and the rest, first presented in his anthologies the poetry of pre-war leftism, an 'engaged' poetry, with its accompanying imagery of an industrial landscape. It was a new vision to which these poets gave expression; and Michael's book on the 'imagist' poetic theory of T. E. Hulme gave definition to an aesthetic which (although nominally Christian) fitted in with the concreteness of the Marxists among them. I was out of my element in that world and began to come into my own only from the time I escaped, not only from

Cambridge, but from the literary values of the 'thirties altogether. That kind of poetry was alien to me; yet the poets of Cambridge (and of these Michael was forerunner) were my first friends. I do not know that Michael would ever have seen altogether what as a poet I was about, even though he did like some of the poems I wrote in those Penrith and Martindale years, and wanted to include some in the revised edition of the anthology he was planning at the time of his death. Subsequently I allowed poems of mine to be included, at Janet's request, in the later edition. For friendship's sake I am glad to be there; but I no more belong with those contemporaries of the 'thirties, with their political idealism and social realist imagery, than with William Empson and his 'metaphysical' (in the literary sense, not the philosophic) positivism; less so, indeed; for with William—as indeed, with Michael himself, who was, like William, a mathematician—I did share something of the inscape of science and its remote images, cold vistas of nature.

Michael saw me differently; he dedicated a poem of his own to me; and shortly before his death he said to Janet, 'K was our beauty.' Our; for, whatever I was, I did belong to my friends in a way I certainly never belonged to husband or lover. I have through 'love' known inspiration and suffering; through friendship, enduring happiness, unalloyed. I will do much for my friends just because no submission is involved. Henry Moore once said to me, in jest, 'I would have made you knuckle under!'—and what man living has more right to pride in the strength of his genius? But in fact not Henry Moore, not Yeats himself could have come between me and that inner companion; no other person's inspiration, however strong, can take the place of our own inner light. Since my marriage with Charles, a fellow-poet, I have never for one moment been tempted to imagine that I could share my interior world in a relationship of marriage, still less sacrifice my anterior dedication *to* a relationship of marriage.

I did not deserve that rescue; I wish I could believe I

have deserved it since. The transformation of my life began, not through my will but through Janet's and Michael's kindness, on the night I stepped out of a dark train into the black-out of Penrith station, with my two weary children. We had travelled from Devonshire, where in my mother's little wooden holiday-hut, looking over the blue sea and cloudless sky of Seaton bay, we had heard Chamberlain's speech declaring this country to be at war with Germany. From the pitch-black night beyond the dim platform came the scent of wet fells, and sheep, and the North; and I knew that after long exile I had come back to my own. The burden and the guilt of years seemed lifted from my heart by that breath from the hills of my childhood.

As we walked in the darkness (Michael, like some Mr. Greatheart, pushing in a perambulator my luggage and my son) I had no idea where we were going or what we would find; and coming out of the dark September night into a gas-lit room in Wordsworth Street, where Janet was, and warmth, and light, was strange and inexplicable as a dream. There is no moment of my life for which I am more deeply grateful; for on the night I stepped out of the darkness into that simple north-country room, so reminiscent of the past, with Janet offering cocoa and her welcoming hands, my own life and my freedom truly began. I had returned to my own country, not now as a country child, but under the protecting friendship of two writers of my own generation.

The house in Wordsworth Street belonged to an old Penrith family related to those Hutchinsons who gave Wordsworth his wife and Coleridge his Asra; and some fragrance of that world remained in those rooms; the Wedgwood jug with ferns, the Birket Foster watercolour over the fireplace of children climbing a stile by a bush of wild roses; the faded green serge table-cloth, the Victorian furniture, reticent but cared for. Just as you will find archaic Greece by walking away from the archaeological sites by any mule-track to the nearest village, so the way into the secret world in which Wordsworth and Dorothy and S.T.C. once lived, closed to professors, is known to maiden ladies

111

who live their lives in the house where they were born. But Janet's Aberdeen was a related place, as was my Northumberland; and she set about living in a country town built of the red local granite as to the manner born. Superimposed upon that older world was ours; Michael's books and his typewriter and gramophone, and the late Beethoven quartets he loved; and our children and all their gear. In that house was friendship of the mind, the best of talk, and the shared tasks of the day; the good life, and how sweet it seemed after such an exile as mine had been.

Pipes froze in that bitter winter; that meant we could not use the boiler; and we had to keep all the water needed for our household of infants in the bath, carrying it in buckets from the main tap in Wordsworth Street, turned on for an hour or two every day. Coal was short; Janet and I did the marketing and cooking in alternate weeks, doing our best with the spam and dried eggs. (As cooks we have both improved beyond recognition since that winter.) In the evenings, when the children were disposed of at last, Janet and I would be sitting by the fire darning and mending, and Michael would come down from his attic study with his pipe and two or three pages of his book, *The Recovery of the West*, or a new poem, and we would talk of literature and the war.

My contributions tended to take the form of large ill-informed generalizations; which Michael would cheerfully demolish with a fact or two. I did not believe that the West would recover; and in my sense of the word recover I was perhaps right; but Michael too was right, at least insofar as England did win that particular war, which at the time seemed unlikely to happen. Mankind, Michael used to say, has a heartening way of never fulfilling predictions based upon logical deductions from existing situations; there are always unexpected turns, and only the unpredictable can be predicted with certainty. Michael perhaps felt as I did, but, like all good educators, understood that even when a civilization is in decline, it is possible to make small improvements wherever we may happen to be, and necessary

112

to confine our hopes to attainable and specific ends, towards which it is in our power to work. Now that I am older I admire with greater understanding the stoicism with which Michael concentrated his hopes and fears within the scope of his own field of action. His practical political sense was in this respect altogether unlike my father's; or, indeed, like those University Marxists I had known who had made of the Spanish Civil War a symbol of their vague Utopia.

Sometimes behind the black-out Janet and Michael would talk of climbs in the French Alps, re-living days of freedom above the snowline of human affairs. There were days, too, when Janet and Michael would go off on mountain walks or climbs in the fells; or I myself, with Janet or Michael, and occasionally all three of us. Once we walked to the summit of Fairfield, in February, perhaps, for the wet snow was melting away in the wind. There was a rainbow that day, against the snow, cast by some trick of light from the spray of a little waterfall, and the track of a fox. With Michael, one ice-cold winter's day, I struggled up Blencathra, where, just under the summit, out of the wind which cut like a knife and rattled the wedges of ice which adhered to the underside of every blade of grass, we ate our frozen sardines and Michael smoked his pipe, before we set off for the descent, through sheltering woods, to Keswick. On the New Year's day of a later year, Janet and I, by contrast, basked in the sunshine on the summit of Helvellyn. On another expedition, when our three eldest children could walk, Michael and I took them up Helvellyn, whose summit was a Brocken of swirling mist. Michael I remember saying to me, as the witch's brew of wind and vapour boiled up from below, 'Just look over, K, will you, and see if you can see Striding Edge.' I could; but fortunately only so much of its jagged back as was bearable. Roped, Michael leading, we took our children across. Such days were essentially of Janet's and Michael's creation; they enjoyed the effort and the victory. Left to myself I never wished to struggle, but only to be forever in the places I loved, to sit hour after hour by waterfall or mossy rock; not to visit but to be

113

eternally (at least for the moment eternally) at one with places remote from the human world. I would rather have been one of those hermits who in some cave of the Himalayas meditated upon transience and *nirvana*, than their European 'conquerors'; but Michael was essentially a conqueror of summits. Whenever I see the constellation of Orion, I think of Michael tirelessly striding ahead of whatever party of us lagged behind.

At the end of the first winter of the war the house in Wordsworth Street was sold by its owners and our household had to leave; the Robertses finding another house in Penrith and I to my appointed place. I decided to look for a cottage, and not knowing where to begin I went one late February morning to the bus terminus in Penrith and took a bus to Howtown, on the eastern and wilder side of Ullswater; for at Martindale my Aunt Peggy Black had taught her first school, more than fifty years before. Because of this, taking that way seemed not like a departure but like a return. Crossing to the little hotel I asked if any cottages were to let in the neighbourhood. 'Only the vicarage,' I was told; and when I replied that the vicarage would be much too big for me, was reassured; the vicarage was very small. Over the fell road I walked, the sweet scent of earliest spring poignant in the soft air into which the snow was melting. Martindale vicarage, the most beautiful little white house imaginable, stood in its own field, with a great lime tree at the gate and a beck fringed with birch and alder bounding its little domain. It stood empty, as if waiting for me. The house, which had a certain elegance of proportion above that of cottage, had a room on each side of the front door and four tiny bedrooms above. Its windows looked south, to Beda Fell and High Street, the frontier never passed by the Roman legions. The garden, enclosed by a stone wall, was sheltered by two spreading yews where a little flock of coal-tits gathered to eat the red berries. On that first sight of it, multitudes of snowdrops were emerging from the melting snow, and the scented buds of the flowering currant bushes were already swelling. A tall window with a semicircular top, of a kind fairly common in Cumberland rose to the whole height of the staircase, looking up the fell-side behind the house where a small rivulet tumbled over its stones and mosses. Often, later, I saw red deer up there, from the Boardale herd, the last in Cumberland.

To the Vicarage I came home to the world I had thought lost to me for ever. It was as if the same multitude of snow-drops had awaited my return, and the sound of the beck that flowed through the field the sound of the same burn flowing all night that I had heard as I lay in my bed in the blue bedroom at the Manse. Again the evenings were lit with Aladdin lamps, again my field and garden were divided from the wild world only by a stone dyke. The formation of the fells is very unlike the great rising sweep of the Northumbrian moors; in every dale there is a boundary, like the mark of a tide, to which has risen the human world of little fields; above the sinuous line of the last stone dyke rises the world beyond the human, stone and sedge and parsley-fern and fell-sheep, curlew and buzzard; but the wilderness, in a different idiom, tells everywhere of the same nature, still virgin as before the Fall of man. I too felt myself, here, to have escaped from mankind, from all those who had, as it seemed to me, hunted me down. I came like a wounded animal at last into the inviolable safety of my own terrain. Free from Cambridge, from marriage, from Mass-Observation and Marxism, from Ilford, the fell-sheep and the birds spoke my own language and of the things I understood; and I seemed virgin again. It seems to me strange now, in retrospect, that no sense of guilt pursued me there or obscured my vision of the purity of the creation but so it was. Perhaps the world of nature not only pro-tected but absolved me; perhaps the penance was only deferred. Perhaps the deeper truth is that nature does not speak of guilt and remorse, only of that dispassionate mind in whose vast peace an infinite complexity of forms waxes and wanes at every moment, held in perfect equilibrium and perfectly present, as if no evil of past or future had power to mar the perfection of the everlasting Now; a now always immaculate, remembering no sorrow, fearing no dissolution, a virginity for ever renewing itself. Over the dead the grass grows again, and nothing is remembered, no memory hunts down the creatures of that eternal present. Into that Now no Eumenides pursued me.

Some of the farmers and their sisters in the dales had been my Aunty Peggy's pupils and still remembered her. How could I not have felt that I had been led into that valley of refuge, and that it was, for me, under a blessing? A Spanish friend has told me of a word, in his language, which means love of that specific kind which draws us back to that place from which we have come; as old people as they approach death long to return to their native place; or as a mortally wounded bull in the bull-ring will attempt to walk in the direction of the field from which it has been brought: *querencia*. Was it this instinct which led me now to Martindale? I began now to perceive that there is a pattern in life, or rather that a life is such a pattern, however obliterated and spoiled, and I felt for the first time since childhood that I had come into my own.

For many who moved from town to country at the beginning of the war, as I did, the change was only of location; for me it was a change of identity, or rather a return to identity. Even for Janet and Michael the mountains they loved were a relaxation from work; *Mountain Holidays*, Janet entitled her book. But for me, in some obscure sense, to live with the natural creation was, at this time, my work. No less surely than in Ilford, and later in my two marriages, I had known I was not where I should be, at Martindale I felt, each day, each hour, that here I was in my own place. I have often since thought psychiatrists waste much effort in trying to 'adjust' unhappy people to some bed of Procrustes, when all they need is to get away and to find, as I did, their right place and their right work. 'Things move violently to their places, smoothly in their places.'

To an outside observer it might have seemed that my troubles had only begun, the struggle to earn enough money to keep myself and my children (Charles could allow me only a small sum) which I did in part by book-reviewing. I had to cook, clean, saw logs, make fires; look after my children, teach them, carry my marketing once a week from Penrith, grow vegetables in the garden. But to me, free now, and in my own place, all this labour was a joy, whereas the ease and apparent freedom of my former life had been, for all the magic of possession by Charles's dream, a sojourn in Hades. There is a difference in kind between the Hells and the Purgatories, even though in these the effort may be greater and the suffering more acute.

Housework had formerly been to me, as to so many unhappy women, a symbol of enslavement; I had seen my mother all her life hating and resenting what she called the 'drudgery' of housework. This irrational resentment of housework is I believe strongly felt by women whose marriages are unhappy. There is at the same time a compulsion to perform the tasks of enslavement; to leave the furniture undusted might be the first act of freedom. My upbringing had strongly impressed on me the sense that there is some moral virtue attaching to the performance of menial tasks, whereas it is 'selfish' to perform tasks not menial; as if my mother were still accusing me of leaving to her the 'drudgery' of Martha. When at Martindale I had to sweep and clean once more I had a momentary return of the old fear of loss of identity, as if the jaws of Ilford yawned to swallow me back. One day soon after I had gone to Martindale I was scrubbing the stone flags of the larder, on my hands and knees, weighed down by this sense of pursuit; I felt that circumstances were robbing me of my identity, so precarious still, as poet, or as whatever it was I hoped to become. Suddenly, as with the shifting of a *gestalt,* I realized that I was the same person whether scrubbing a floor or writing a poem; that my dignity as a being was in no way dependent upon the role which I had at any moment to assume; for all such roles are merely that, and the person free of them all. I became, from that moment, free of the act; and I have never from that day minded any form of necessary work. Perhaps I have minded too little; to me housework and the like has not been so much a burden as a subtle form of sloth, a temptation to put the less before the more important task. It is all too easy, especially for women, to put the less essential physical task before the more essential intangible work; Martha is always self-righteous in her tyranny over Mary. Thus it was that for so many years, before I permitted myself to write a poem, I would feel compelled to complete all my domestic tasks, even down to darning the last pair of children's socks in my work-basket.

I lived, then, during that summer when France fell, in a state and place where all was radiant with that interior light of which Traherne has written; and beyond the continuous interior illumination of moss and fern, of yellow welsh poppies and water flowing over stones reflecting the glitter of pure light, the warmth of the sun on the stone seat under the yew-tree, the scent of young birch-leaves and lime-blossom, the line of the fells ever changing in sun and shadow, certain moments there were of another kind of consciousness altogether. Such a state has been often enough described: Tennyson said he could enter it at will; Richard Jeffries and others have known it well. 'Nature mysticism' occupies, it may be, a relatively humble place on the ladder of perfection as compared with those states of consciousness attained by saints and sages; but as compared with normal consciousness the difference is as between the world and paradise, if indeed it be not precisely that. Descriptions of one state of consciousness in terms of another must, to those who have not themselves known the experience, always give the impression of being figurative or poetic; so it always must be when, in whatever field, ignorance passes judgement upon knowledge. But those who know are unanimous in reporting that such changes of consciousness are not of degree, but of kind; not some strong emotion or excitement but a clarity in which all is minutely perceived as if by finer sense.

I kept always on the table where I wrote my poems a

bowl with different beautiful kinds of moss and lycopodium and long and deeply did I gaze at those forms, and into their luminous smaragdine green. There was also a hyacinth growing in an amethyst glass; I was sitting alone, in an evening, at my table, the Aladdin lamp lit, the fire of logs burning in the hearth. All was stilled. I was looking at the hyacinth, and as I gazed at the form of its petals and the strength of their curve as they open and curl back to reveal the mysterious flower-centres with their anthers and eye-like hearts, abruptly I found that I was no longer looking *at* it, but *was* it; a distinct, indescribable, but in no way vague, still less emotional, shift of consciousness into the plant itself. Or rather I and the plant were one and indistinguishable; as if the plant were a part of my consciousness. I dared scarcely to breath, held in a kind of fine attention in which I could sense the very flow of life in the cells. I was not perceiving the flower but living it. I was aware of the life of the plant as a slow flow or circulation of a vital current of liquid light of the utmost purity. I could apprehend as a simple essence formal structure and dynamic process. This dynamic form was, as it seemed, of a spiritual not a material order; or of a finer matter, or of matter itself perceived as spirit. There was nothing emotional about this experience which was, on the contrary, an almost mathematical apprehension of a complex and organized whole, apprehended *as* a whole. This whole was living; and as such inspired a sense of immaculate holiness. Living form—that is how I can best name the essence or soul of the plant. By 'living' I do not mean that which distinguishes animal from plant or plant from mineral, but rather a quality possessed by all these in their different degrees. Either everything is, in this sense, living, or nothing is; this negation being the view to which materialism continually tends; for lack, as I now knew, of the immediate apprehension of life, as life. The experience lasted for some time—I have no idea how long— and I returned to dull common consciousness with a sense of diminution. I had never before experienced the like, nor have I since in the same degree; and yet it seemed at the time not strange but infinitely familiar, as if I were experiencing at last things as they are, was where I belonged, where in some sense, I had always been and would always be. That almost continuous sense of exile and incompleteness of experience which is, I suppose, the average human state, was gone like a film from sight. In these matters to know once is to know for ever. My mother when she was over eighty confided to me an experience she had had as a girl. 'I have never told anyone before,' she said, 'but I think you will understand.' It was simply that, one day, sitting among the heather near Kielder 'I saw that the moor was alive.' That was all. But I understood that she had seen what I had seen.

All traditions speak of the greater beauty and clarity of visionary forms; and this must be so, not because these are an 'idealization' of nature, but because souls are those forms of which physical embodiments are but a signature, sometimes almost indecipherable. It is not by chance that the art of a spiritual civilization is characterized by the lucidity of its forms; those six-armed dancing Shivas, rhythmic in every contour, or those sculptured women, perfected in the utmost refinement of eroticism, who keep the doors of Indian temples; or Christian angels with their braided hair and features delicately traced on skies of gold. When natural forms are depicted, as in Gothic foliate sculpture, or the flowers of the Cluny tapestries, or the fish and birds of the Book of Kells, these have the clarity, freshness and perfection of spiritual vision, for it is the souls of plant or animal whose clear lineaments are traced, in all their delicate mathematical intricacy. Paradoxically it is naturalistic art which loses the very form it seeks to copy; materialism makes a chaos of, precisely, the material world.

At about the time of my hyacinth vision I had an immediate experience of what might be the human equivalent of the plant-soul I had perceived. I was lying in bed, thinking, no doubt, of my absent lover. I say this lest it should be thought that my experience was in any way religious or related to prayer or to moral virtue. Abruptly, although my

120

physical body was lying down, I found myself, at the same time, sitting upright, my arms outstretched: but not my physical arms. This body which seemed to have emerged from within the physical envelope like a moth from a chrysalis seemed infinitely more myself than the physical envelope which it had left. It had a sense of lightness, clarity and freedom, a freshness comparable with the flower as I had seen it: not at all like that shadowy tenuous self we are in dreams. All seemed not less but more clear, of a quality more real than the real. So surprised was I to find myself half out of my body that I found myself back in it again. The return to the physical body was like putting on some old sack, rough and crude and barely conscious, constricted and dull; this has never happened to me since, but again, once is enough. 'As dreamers wake from sleep we wake from waking.' So I years later expressed this experience in a line of a poem; words not figurative.

Another insight is more difficult to describe, because it was an intuition purely qualitative; as a thought, most elementary, but as an apprehension, transforming. Truth, truism—words themselves mean nothing, but are only signs pointing to things perceived and experienced. Sometimes in remote places one still meets virtually illiterate people whose words are laden with living content, full of resonances; and the shock throws into contrast the fading of meaning from current language, not so much by the diminishing of vocabulary as by the thinning of the words themselves. Therefore I can only remotely indicate, not define, an apprehension which was transforming. It came from the wind, which blows with such unbroken force down the dales; the incessant rain drifting like a curtain; and along with the flow of wind the flow of water in the beck, swollen with all the rivulets of the fells, pouring itself towards the lake. It was a realization of the *Tao,* one might say, of the power of the elements finding their way not by effort but by effortlessness. I saw that human beings are forever striving against the great current on which we are carried, whose power is so immeasurably great that in

121

resisting we can destroy only ourselves; but if we go with it, that strength is ours, that energy sustains us.

Perhaps as a corollary to this realization that our only strength is that of the great tides and forces of the cosmos, it occurred to me at about that time that one might pray. My reasoning was simple: if there are no winds and currents of spiritual energy, the attempt could harm no one but would merely be ineffectual; whereas if there are it would be foolish not to take advantage of them. Prayer could only do nothing, or do good: it could do no harm. So simple an empiricism one might expect to have occurred to more people than seems to be the case. Professed agnostics seem not to be experimental, and wait for their doubts to be removed before putting them to the only tests which could remove them.

At Martindale vicarage I shared with my children many things. We lived in the Westmorland of Beatrix Potter, weaving a world of the real and the here and now about our coal-tits and rabbits, our white cat, the dipper's nest under the bridge, the log-fire and bramble-jelly and toast for tea. We had a natural history museum on the landing, where caterpillars, supplied with their food-plant (nettles) presently performed for us their metamorphosis into chrysalids, and later hatched into peacock butterflies. I shared with them songs from the Baby's Opera, and the Père Castor nature-books, and Edward Thompson Seton and all the old fairy-books and myths. I thought our shared world was a happy one; but my daughter tells me she was never happy as a child. I thought my anxieties and in-security were hidden from my children, but from child-hood nothing is hidden, they see the reality, not the mask we wear, even though it is our love for them that makes us wear the mask. I withheld myself to protect both them and myself from my own secret inner wounds; but also because I was passionately in love with a man other than their father; and by that passion my imagination was absorbed, to their exclusion. This dream nourished my poetry; but it did not nourish Charles's children. To all outward appearance I did my best for them; but the inner reality was otherwise. I did not give my children any part of my spiritual life. In this I greatly wronged them, depriving them of what as a child had been given to me so fully in the undivided world of Bavington; I gave part of myself wholly, but it would have been better to give the whole of myself partly. It was as if I were two people, the poet, who existed in solitude, and another person. The habit of keeping hidden all that was vital to the poet had come perhaps from my past, when I had somehow to elude my father's moral and religious dominance, and my mother's hungry emotion, or perish.

Yet in the solitude of my interior world, whose sanctuary I had at last succeeded in securing against those who would, knowingly or unknowingly, have destroyed it, I lived in continuous delight; the poems I then wrote seem too meagre a gleaning from those fields of paradise. In that interior world my real life was lived; I was almost continuously aware of my daimon, and passing spirits of the elements came and went. It is to me most mysterious that I was permitted, as poet, this vision of paradise, while as a woman I was in so many ways blameworthy. Why was I, absorbed as I was by an illicit and unrequited love, allowed to remain in Eden? Is it possible that a state of passionate love is not only innocent, but a return to the state of innocence itself? I do not know; at the time I had no sense of guilt; I did not think about myself or my moral state at all, but only of what I saw and knew of nature in the deep look I then took into its sanctuaries; and love, even upon the most carnal level, does, it seems, give wings that carry us above the world of guilt into a state of perception in which all is transfigured into the beautiful and the holy. The few poems I then wrote, fragile as they were, reflect, perhaps, an illumination from a world or state which lies beyond and above the egoism of guilt and sorrow. Perhaps a polytheist would have better understood these contradictions; as in the Greek myths some have received the mysteries of Dionysus, frowned on by Hera; or Zeus might bless while

Demeter's fields lay barren; or Aphrodite destroy the follower of Artemis the upright. I can see now that I had no right to be so happy; yet I was permitted to be.

Martindale was an experience of solitude; solitude, but not loneliness; for solitude is the most intensely experienced state. Boredom in solitude is to me unimaginable; are we not bored only in the enforced company of the wrong people? People, that is, in whose company we cannot be our true selves? From the intensity of my inner life I had to emerge when human friends visited me.

For into my sanctuary—and during the war the country reverted to what it had been thirty years before, when there were no cars, or few—some friends did penetrate. Janet and Michael of course; and the house in Penrith to which they had now moved (Penrith took on, from my remote dale, the dimensions and qualities of a capital city) was my one point of attachment to the outer world. Once William Empson came with Michael, entirely and in all simplicity as he had been on his window-sill in Magdalene, or in Marchmont Street where, perched on a three-legged chair whose broken fourth was propped by the *Tale of Genji*, he had read me some quotation from a book whose place was marked by a dry kipper-bone. So entirely was he as he would have been anywhere and under any circumstances, that I felt strangely reassured that I myself had not altogether ceased to be the person of my earlier and better Cambridge days. Nature protected me; but I was grateful, also, to my friends for not forgetting me.

William was wearing a strange glossy black waterproof garment, which enhanced that sense of shock which his presence always produced; he had bought it in Hanoi, where he had worn it, very likely, during the great retreat into the interior before the advancing Japanese, in which he had accompanied his students of Pekin University. He was also wearing two left shoes that day, absentmindedly picked up as he dressed for a walk across the fells with Michael (they were going to to climb Great Gable). He confessed to the blisters only afterwards. Not only is William

124

the same against any background, he assumes that his friends are. I could not have explained to him, even had I wished to do so, that in Martindale I was not the girl he had known, for this would have meant nothing to him; and therefore became, in relation to William, untrue. As with my parents I remained the daughter they saw in me, so with friends I found myself adopting the *persona* under which they had known me; only alone was I, at that time, able to be the self I really was. This remained so for many years to come; may even be so now. The only way to be rid of the disguise was to be rid of the situation which forced me to adopt it.

William Empson is just the opposite. It was not that he was a townsman out of place among rocks and stones and trees; he is after all a countryman born, and had ridden to hounds, so we always understood, in his native Yorkshire. But environment was indifferent to him, because his mind was so much its own place that he perhaps never noticed any other; possibly because he was short-sighted and always wore strong glasses. My invisible companions, my nature-spirits silently withdrew before William. Boehme says that spirits of different natures may occupy the same place but will even so remain invisible to one another, each being in its own universe; so it was that William never saw my secret world. Nevertheless I was glad to see William.

I walked with William and Michael by the lake side as far as Patterdale; it grew hot, I remember, and I took off my woollen jacket. William offered to carry it for me, with the simplicity of his good manners; but I, instinctively too, said no, I could perfectly well carry it myself. 'Of course that is what you would say,' William remarked with one of his very rare excursions into the personal. I thought as I walked back alone of William's picture of me as someone who could carry her own jacket and refuse the simplest of civilities; out of the pride of the humbly born who cannot accept favours? Out of mistrust of the slightest gesture which might arouse my suspicion of the fowler's net? I had been too easily hunted down; now I had grown wary, adept

125

at evading, like a seed of thistledown which floats away on the slightest movement of air made by the motion of the capturing hand.

William's sister-in-law and her two children had rented a house near Pooley Bridge; and Monica Empson visited me and offered to allow my daughter to share her children's governess, an act of kindness which I gratefully did accept. Monica Empson was one of those who, in changing her location had not changed her world; and I envied her secure place in the social order; for I had none, not even the magical status of poet—or scarcely so, for I had barely begun to write and publish. Strong as I felt myself to be in the company of the birds and weather of the fells, I knew myself weak and vulnerable in all relationships with my own species. It was for William's sake that Monica accepted me; William who remained in his own secure world of the Yorkshire gentry in spite of being a poet. That world, indeed, tolerates such eccentricities in the family; and I wished I had such firm ground under my feet. Even in bohemia it remained firm under William's feet; such as he cannot lose caste.

In order to make ends meet, and also because in those war years accommodation in the country was scarce, I took into the vicarage a mother with two little girls. The arrangement worked well enough; we shared the cooking and the little school (helped by the PNEU syllabus, which we dutifully followed) and one of our pleasant arrangements was that from time to time she or I would take a week-end away. It is hard now to recapture the sense of distance from the world in which we then lived in our valley; war had sealed us off in our pleasant sanctuary, so that Penrith was the only town left in our world; London had vanished over the rim of space. To me this was an unimaginable blessing, as if with London all my unhappy past had disappeared out of the universe. So it was that country neighbours became, as before the motor-car, a closed society, dependent upon one another, and making plans to meet a long time ahead (we had no telephone either) and with a sense of the great importance of small events. Perhaps we touched again, in that isolation, a lost human norm, seeing one another more justly in that oasis of permanence. It was as if we would always be there, like the fells, Janet at Penrith, I at Martindale; and yet we were only there by grace of the abnormal conditions of war.

So it was that my first invitation to visit Cockley Moor was an event almost unimaginable. Martindale had become my whole world; nor did it seem a small world, but rather an infinite one, in which each day was unique, not one moment to be lost; for rain and sunlight came and went, always some tree was budding, some flower opening. To go away even for two days was to miss some event of nature; the house-martins in the eaves leaving their nests, or deer coming down from the fells, or a white luminous ring round the sun, or the first wood-anemones or the last golden day of autumn warm enough for tea on the stone table under the yew.

Through Janet and Michael it was that I first met the friend who from that time to the end of her life was to be my wise counsellor; without whose practical help and charitable forbearance (I use those Christian words for she was a church-woman) I cannot imagine how I could have survived the years that followed. Helen Christian Sutherland, patron of the arts and of artists, Janet had met in Newcastle and visited at Rock Hall. Now she had moved to a new house, at Matterdale; one of the two highest inhabited houses in England, it was said.

The day of my visit to Cockley Moor was one of those days of steady drifting rain that are so beautiful in those hills, enclosing all in still deeper secrecy behind the curtain of falling water. It did not seem to me in any way strange to set out to walk on such a day; for I had been a child in just such a place, and walking still seemed to me the obvious means of coming and going. My father had had no car, nor had Charles after our marriage; I have never had a car, and, apart from the convenience of rapid transport, detest motoring, for, accustomed as I have been to being in places and not merely passing through them, motoring is for me a continual sense of being swept past and away from that in which I would wish to be. To walk in the rain, because this is necessary and natural, because one lives in a world of nature of which rain and snow are as much a part as sun and moon, is part of a lost heritage.

I had packed in my ruck-sack, wrapping it in many layers against the wet, some sort of evening-dress kept from a former life, and dressed myself for the long walk through the drifting incessant curtain of south-westerly rain, soft in my face and bringing out all the delicate scents of the fell, of moss and birch-leaves and sheep, distilled on the tongue like the pure essence of the element of water. As I walked up Boardale and into the loneliness I seemed to have left even Martindale behind me, to be restored to the simplicity of the alone with the Alone; that was the condition I was always seeking, to be cleansed by rain and wind, washed clean of myself; and so, deserved or undeserved, it was; for the elements of nature take no account of moral deserts, refusing none. I seemed, I remember, almost to be walking into the very being of the elementals of the hills and the clouds, out of the human condition altogether; and then, over the pass, to descend again into a world whose frontiers were mysteriously closed, and mud and stone and rain all once again measured by human standards; as cold, inconvenient and dirty.

Helen Sutherland had driven to Patterdale to meet me; and well she might have rejected the shabby figure streaming with wet; but instead she took me into her immaculate car (she was reading the latest volume of the the Faber poets, a translation of Virgil by C. Day Lewis, I seem to remember) and we were driven to Cockley Moor. There, for the first time since the outbreak of war, or indeed long before that, I found myself in a house which seemed to me then more like a place of the imagination—some castle in Spenser (the elegant Spenser rather than the puritan Bunyan), one of those places of arrival where treasures are shown to pilgrim or traveller, and wounds are healed.

'Tout était une rhythme et une rite et une cérémonie, depuis le petit lever,' so begins the passage of Péguy which hung in the hall (lettered by Helen's god-daughter, Nicolete Gray); I had come from the world of nature into the world of art, another universe. In this house whose very cleanliness was a luxury, whose library of books Victorian and new, whose famous collection of paintings, Seurat and Ben Nicholson, Courbet and Mondrian, David Jones and Christopher Wood and even (in a cupboard for she did not care for them) two Picassos, I was lifted as by a tide above the mean struggle of poverty, to wake next morning in the peace of a spotless white room. Here I was made to feel that the poet in me was a being of worth, of whom much was hoped and expected, who had something to contribute to this world of excellence; whose poems might somehow justify and redeem my existence. Helen Sutherland saved me from bohemia; but for her I should, as a poet, have had no other ground beneath my feet. By her I was given the dignity accorded to poets in former times and in other countries, but seldom in modern England; and access to the great world and its values. For by the measure of perfection all art is finally tested and proved, and not by majority opinion or the fashion of little groups. It is a loss to any artist to have no access to an aristocracy (using the word in Plato's sense), whose function it is to keep alive those values; the pearls and not the acorns, food of natural mankind. The ill effects of this want have disastrously lowered the standards by which works are judged and to which, therefore, they tend to conform, in writers of the post-war generation, less fortunate than mine in the far lower level of culture in the world from which they draw their sustenance and for which they write. 'Conduct and work grow coarse, and coarse the soul' for the lack of a context, an environment of thought and feeling of a certain quality and discrimination which can only be preserved by a class both leisured and learned. For feeling too has its culture. Fineness of feeling requires a freedom and privacy accorded to few in the modern world, to look, to

listen, to think without anxiety or self-interest; learning too demands leisure, both to acquire and to disseminate; and the struggle for survival produces many mental distortions.

Of musicians and painters Helen Sutherland had long been a patron; the Bush quartet used to play for her musical parties in London. Vera Moore, the pianist, was her special protégée; from David Jones, from Ben and Winifred Nicholson, from Naum Gabo, long before these were famous (as later from Barbara Hepworth) she had bought their best works; for her judgement of particular works was as discerning as her judgement of the artists themselves. Leslie Martin, then almost unknown, designed the new wing she had added to the old stone farm-house of Cockley Moor. Three generations of Binyons and Bosanquets and Hodgkins had been her friends and many of them her godchildren; Lord Gray of Fallodon and Sir William Beveridge among her close friends; these and many more, serious scholars or fine artists. I first met the poet Norman Nicholson at her house, and, nearing the end of her life, she could not refrain from adding one more to the number of her chosen—the poetess Elizabeth Jennings.

Of all these she was more than a purchaser of finished works; David Jones stayed with her at Rock for long periods of work, and painted again—though less happily, for those bare fells were without the dimension of legend or history his imagination needed—at Cockley Moor. Friend, counsellor, perfectionist, she called out in all whom she admitted into her circle of friends in whose work she believed, by a combination of entire imaginative sympathy and exacting attention to detail, their best work, and, upon visits, their best behaviour.

Perhaps only David Jones could in her eyes do no wrong; but it is characteristic of both that even he was on more than one occasion caught in a kind of fatality of mishaps in her house (in the style of P. G. Wodehouse whom she also admired, and allowed to her guests, as she did her good wine, in small amounts, and on proper occasions; for in her

130

library she kept, besides the best and most recent works on history, theology, art, poetry, gardening, and cookery, a chosen shelf of books for pleasure and relaxation).

Once when we were both staying at Cockley Moor David came to find me, much shaken; what should he do, he had spilt a bottle of ink down the immaculate white wall of his bedroom. For a whole day he laid aside the painting on which he was at work to obliterate the damning blot, and late in the afternoon summoned me to see whether any trace could still be detected. He told me how at Rock, perhaps on his first visit, he had, on his arrival in another room whose perfection had reproached him, caught sight of himself in the glass, and had, like Tom the chimney-sweep in Ellie's bedroom, been overcome with shame: obviously his hair must be cut at once. Another guest, a young woman to whom this predicament could be confided, was summoned; she agreed to cut his hair, but how prevent the clippings from falling onto that spotless floor? They arrived at the solution of taking a sheet from the bed to catch the hair, which she then snipped off. But then, how to get rid of it? Together they carried the sheet into the private wood behind the house, only to meet Helen approaching down a walk where she had been feeding her birds. There was nothing to be done but to confess: why had David not told her, the chauffeur could have driven him to the barber, etc., etc. But how well I could understand the paralysing sense of shortcoming that at times I think has overcome us all in Helen's house. I remember Lord Beveridge being scolded most severely for coming in two minutes late for lunch; and there was something about a distinguished Benedictine monk and a hot-water-bottle (Helen often gave to her friends copies of the Rule of St. Benedict, which makes no mention of hot-water-bottles) and Jim Ede picking a forbidden carnation.

Another memory of David Jones comes back to me; in which I seemed to see at once the human vulnerability and the artist's knowledge that his work has moved away from him into a life of its own, into another order of things.

Among Helen's collection was David's portrait of Eric Gill's daughter, *Petra in Rosenhag*. It must have been put away (why? Did it speak too clearly and nearly the language of love for Helen's own hurt to be able to sustain it?) for David had got it out, and propped it against a chair in the drawing-room. I remember that I came into the room, and saw David there, alone, looking at the painting. Was he communing with memory or with art? I felt I had intruded, but could not instantly withdraw; and received the pondering sweetness of the look no other person had been meant to see.

Her perfectionism did not begin or end with the fine arts; it was therefore inescapable. Clothes, cookery and domestic economy, wine, textiles, flowers, dog-biscuits, bird-food and the clergy, all must come up to that exacting standard of hers, 'The best *is* the best.' As an Anglican, her only hesitation was as to whether Rome '*is* the best'; but, born to rule, her father's daughter (her father was Sir Arthur Sutherland of the P. and O. Shipping Company) she never submitted to the Bishop of Rome. But she liked others to be Catholics; Nicolete Gray and David Jones were, for her, in this sense, 'the best'. She would have made the greatest of all Tudor monarchs, uniting with the administrative economy of Henry VII the learning of Edward VI, Elizabeth's feminine power of evoking from her courtiers and artists 'the best'; and something of the writing on Mary Tudor's heart.

Helen Sutherland was for me from that time on what better poets than I have often lacked, a friend and protector of whatever small flame was alight in me. There are such things as spiritual friends, friends of the genius rather than of the natural creature it inhabits; and such was Helen Sutherland to me. Because she believed in that small flame of mine she tended and tolerated the rest of me, the wretched young woman whose shortcomings well might have made her reject the whole. This she did with a gentleness which yet never became that facile acceptance of anything and everything, which is the bohemian counterfeit of true kindness. Always she applied (and this with her mind above all) the first principles of Christian morality to each specific situation; having reached a conclusion as to 'the best' in this sense, her counsel or her help would follow. Instinctively she had, besides, a sense of the dimension of time which brings to fruition what is in us; and having decided that poetry was in me, she was prepared to wait, and to tolerate. Never did she reproach me for my sins; only for my faults—for not turning my mattress daily, or for leaving an electric light on in the passage outside my bedroom, or taking too much hot water for my bath; but never for leaving my husband, for my inability to cope with my life, or for being in love.

Her gentleness to suffering, however deserved and self-caused (my own, for instance, but I was not the first of her friends in the world of the arts to have entangled my life) her tolerance of the larger sins and mistakes, was boundless. In some despairing phase I said to her once that I was a failure, and had not and never now would, write the poems I should and could have written; and she replied, gently and severely, 'Well, I have sometimes been told that I am a very good judge, and I think you will.' For although she could not help exerting power, she was, at the same time, entirely responsive to whatever each of her friends had to bring. After dinner she would settle in her chair, her dogs at her feet, a piece of embroidery or exquisite mending in her bird-like hands, attentive; if I had new poems, she would listen to them; ask me to re-read, to explain. She would listen, with the same attention, to a young student testing his political or vocational ideas and ideals, as to David Jones or Ben Nicholson. Or she would let us choose some book to read aloud—on consecutive evenings, if we were making a long stay—Dante or Wordsworth, or T. S. Eliot (or sometimes Mrs. Gaskell or P. G. Wodehouse) or Vera Moore would play Mozart and Bach and Couperin.

In how many memories besides mine Helen's drawing-room, designed by Leslie Martin before he became famous (for Helen recognized talent before others did, and was indifferent to reputation, trusting in her own judgement) still exists as it was! It seemed as if, with sun and moon rising and setting over High Street and the sweep of the fells, crossed by moving cloud and cloud-shadows, or sweeping rain, the outer world beyond the uncurtained window that ran the full length of the south-facing wall, was brought within the compass of Helen's civilizing power. To me, the wilds were, and ever will be, places of refuge from the human. But from Helen's drawing-room, thrice distilled, those bare hills and wet clouds, the moon and the stars, became a part of the world of art she had created. Now that room is gone; each thing from its place, where it had seemed to belong as perfectly as every subtle brush-stroke of colour in a painting. Seeing again, long after, on a visit to Edinburgh, two of Helen's Ben Nicholsons in the little museum of modern art in the Botanic Gardens, I was suddenly taken back, in memory, into that vanished room where for so long they hung. The little Seurat too is in Edinburgh; the Winifred Nicholson of Bank's Head in the Kettle's Yard museum in Cambridge; also built by Leslie Martin, and reflecting in its taste much that Helen had originated. I can open the door, in memory, now, and move round that room, touching bookcase, chair and desk; the velvet cloth on the grand piano; the lyre-shaped music-stand; Helen's desk, scattered with her papers, where she wrote to us those inimitable letters in her fine hand, with their added parentheses and insertions and afterthoughts; her own armchair with its reading-lamp with her work-table at hand, and the little pile of *The Times* she never threw away unread, cutting out paragraphs on theology, or nature, or the arts, to send to friends or to keep. The gramophone with its great horn, on which she would sometimes play to us records of Beethoven's or Eliot's quartets; the jars of nuts for the birds and the special dog-biscuits. Over the fire-place the two Persian miniatures that (with her Persian carpets) perhaps celebrated her friendship with Lawrence Binyon; and below them three crystal goblets, and two small Ben Nicholsons; oddly assorted it might seem, but 'the best' of one culture is never out of place beside 'the best' of another. On a round table were displayed the newest books by friends. The very books on the shelves whether history, poetry, theology, cookery or art, their covers immaculate, I could, in memory, still find in their appointed places.

Her pictures, that great, yet most personal collection, still (but for a few donations) intact, belong now to Nicolete Gray; but to Helen's friends they hang, still, in their old places. The great dark Ben Nicholson of interlocking profiles at the end of the room; the romantic early Ben Nicholsons and the later abstracts; the Winifred Nicholson of a white hyacinth against snow; the Cecil Collins pencil drawing; the Italian landscapes by Lelia Caetani, Helen's neighbour since her marriage to Hubert Howard of Lyulph's Tower. Her collection included 'Sunday paintings' by a group of coal-miners in Ashington, valued with the rest; and in valuing their vision and buying their paintings, was she not giving to these also something no social reformer or politician could give? And above all those superb David Joneses, many of them painted at Rock, and some of the fell-side outside the window; and others, of flowers in those very glass vases in which Helen so inimitably arranged winter shoots or spring buds. With its immaculate white walls and the finest works of contemporary artists, that vanished room was the creation of the period and the school of painting of which Helen herself had been the first, as she was to remain the most discriminating, patron. Henry James (her beautiful set of his works is now in the London Library) would have found in her all he most valued. Perhaps he helped to create her.

I saw that room dismantled; first the pictures, then the furniture, piece by piece. I myself heaped on the floor shelf-loads of books, as Helen, confined to her room upstairs, took her leave of them, selecting a few to keep in the nursing home where she went to end her life; relinquishing her possessions with a wave of her hand: 'away, away!' Some went to libraries; some to booksellers; some to friends. I have the set of Balzac that had been her father's; neither library nor bookseller wanted them.

I have written more of my poems on the white window-sill of her little guest-room than in any other house save one.

Helen Sutherland was already grey when I met her; and once I saw her on her terrace, leaning on her stick, a bird-like fragile figure of age, and she seemed in that moment an embodiment of the wisdom of time and of all that matures slowly: of all that is comprised in the astrological figure of Saturn who slowly brings all things to their fulfilment. I understood through her that art is the 'foster-child of silence and slow time'; in her house were many clocks and chronometers soberly measuring the hours, but those hours seemed longer than elsewhere, for work and thought, for reading and writing. She loved, too, the great clock-face of the heavens, 'the heavenly bodies', as she liked to call them, who moved so clear and pure over her high sky; Coleridge's moon, Wordsworth's one star that often shines in the morning or evening sky, in the dawn and twilight already in Cumberland gradual and northern, approaching a little the gloaming of Scotland. During the war, too, the stars seemed more in evidence, being the only lights in the night sky; and at Cockley Moor we seemed almost to touch them; not a light in the village or on the road, and nothing above us but Orion and the constellations. Last thing at night Helen would always let the dogs out, and look at the stars, and at the moon. She always knew from *The Times* charts of the heavens which constellation and planets were to be seen in that clear sky, and loved especially the new moon. How often, dressed in hooded cloak and fur-lined boots, a stick so as not to slip on the ice, Helen would lead me out onto her terrace to look up at the new moon, or the Pleiades; and then, returned, she would make me take down Coleridge's diaries, and read to her those passages about the moon as he had, not long before as star-time goes, watched its passing over neighbouring hills.

Yet in Helen's house, nature was outside, valued as a kind of art, a divine art it may be, but yet not as at Martindale, where I lived within its mystery, and not as its spectator. As a country child I had known that *participation mystique*, as

136

perhaps all country people do, or did, or many among them, the very young or the very old, or those gifted with the kind of sensibility which in other classes would lead to learning or the arts. It is my birthright; and at Martindale I resumed what was to me natural, but now with words and some knowledge which might make it possible to express what every hare in its form or curlew in its nest on the moor perhaps knows but does not know it knows.

In Helen Sutherland's house I was in some respects like an amphibious creature breathing air, and needing to plunge back into my own element. I remember the beauty of the New Year's day of 1940 we all spent with her, I and my children and Janet and Michael and their children, and the little evacuated Newcastle boys whom she had with her; turkey and Christmas pudding, golden angels and silver stars, all rare and precious, with that kind of Christian aestheticism associated with the word 'Anglo-Catholic'. And I remember on another winter day she had given a concert for a pianist also stranded in the North because of the war. It was balm and beatitude to be transported, once again, from cottage to palace, from the world of nature to the world of art, from the struggle to realize anything whatever, to Helen's house of 'the best', where all was achieved, had already undergone its assumption 'out of nature'. Yet of that day of the concert I remember most clearly of all the moment when her car set us down at the gate of the field at Martindale. The moon must have been up, as well as the stars, for there was a birch-tree, entirely encrusted in frozen snow or crystals of ice, and these glittered in the moon-light, green and blue and white. That tree stood in another ground from those forms in which art seeks to embody mere glimpses of a mystery unfathomable; beyond art, so I felt; beyond anything knowable by man. Beyond those limiting frontiers I came into my own again. Returning to that tree I seemed liberated as into a universe upon another scale, beyond all formulations.

Sometimes, too, Helen would visit me, walking along the lake-side path from Patterdale, and I, alone or with my children, would walk to meet her, past the flowering wild-cherry trees of Sandwick, past the slender high waterfall of Scale Howe, past the oak-wood and the birch-wood to the empty fell-side where only juniper bushes grow. There would be a picnic, or return to the vicarage; so on my side of Ullswater I, on behalf of the wild places, received Helen as my guest.

In Helen's house, or with her or through her, I was to meet for the first time many of my most valued friends; David Jones; Hubert and Lelia Howard; Winifred Nicholson who had also been a child of northern hills. She had loved the same wild flowers as I, seen in the hedges of Cumberland the same cranesbill and harebell, scabious and water-avons as I, only a few miles away, in Northumberland. When first I had seen her paintings at an exhibition in London I had wondered how she knew what I thought no one but myself had, in quite that way, seen. When I met her, I understood. From opposite ends of the social scale (she was born in Naworth Castle) we had shared the same beauty, under the same skies. No work could be in greater contrast with Ben Nicholson's abstract period than Winifred's; his with masterly intellectual assurance, hers with the delicate immediacy of feeling; and yet, when he, Winifred and Christopher Wood were working together, there was a quality of feeling in Ben's work which, for all his later mastery, it perhaps later lost. And Winifred, for many years after their separation, could not find the vision those three had shared before Christopher Wood's death, and Ben's departure. Ben (I always thought of him as an elf-man, untouched by human joys and sorrows) was never troubled by remorse, however. When he was about to leave Barbara Hepworth, his second wife, I remember saying to him, in what I intended as reproach, 'You know Ben, you have been married to two very remarkable women.' 'Yes, I know,' said Ben. 'From Winifred I learned a great deal about colour, and from Barbara about form.' So much for marriages. Yet that ruthless integrity of the artist which was for Ben his only law, Helen supremely admired. So, for that matter, did Winifred, for all it had cost her in human sorrow. And so, God knows, do I. I remember when, later, I was wandering in London's hells again, saying to Ben that I could not write, I was too unhappy. He replied, 'When I am happy I use my happiness for my work; when I am unhappy I use my unhappiness.' So surely do all great artists. But I was always too easily overset, falling between the duties of woman and poet and too often failing in both.

To remain for ever, to put down the roots of my life in the place I love, has always been the mirage which I have followed. No more at Martindale than at Bavington did I recognize as a mirage this dream, so securely did the here and now seem to uphold its field and barn, its little parlour and its stone-flagged kitchen, its garden fragrant with flowering-currant and box. I forgot my being there at all was only by grace of an abnormal situation, the war. For the time I remained there my valley had the quality of being for ever, the trees and the beck, the line of hills and the log fire, circumference and centre; and yet the decision to leave was my own.

I began to realize, uneasily, though I was still far from realistic, and still imagined that it must be possible to live by being a poet, that sooner or later I would have to face the problem of earning a living. It seemed to me that in London I could hope to make my way in something I pleased to think of as 'the literary world'; not realizing that the world of those who make a living by writing for the newspapers (whether weekly or daily) has no more to do with the fountains of poetry than has any other profession undertaken in order to make a living. I had, in Janet and Michael, in Helen Sutherland, encountered the values only of 'the best' and because the best valued me, I supposed that to pass muster among the second-best would be easier. What a mistake! I should have been more proud, or more humble; for the only humility I ever had was a false one, an overwhelming diffidence, not in the company of 'the best' (where I have always found understanding) but of the public world, where I have not.

I wonder, now, what I would have done had I possessed even the smallest assured income, the guarantee of the freedom of the merest subsistence? I might have stayed at least a little longer; given to my children a few more years of childhood; possibly; though what is the use of speculating upon hypothetical possibilities? Yet I believe the chief instability of the situation was in myself; the deepest reason for my departure was the unrest which drove me in search of my lover, for whom my passion, in those years of absence, had only increased as it became more imaginary. I was living, in imagination, an ordeal of fidelity, of that keeping faith with the absent which is one of woman's age-old tasks; and as ordeal and task I experienced it, building every day, as a bird builds a nest according to an innate pattern, a beautiful edifice of love, an edifice into which I wove every perception, every thought; which, had it been for a husband whose return I awaited, and not for an empty dream, would have been no different. An instinct of constancy and a strength of something which, if not true love, must surely be one of its components, in me was all misdirected upon a mirage. I explored, in absence, all the imaginative vistas of love. Reading, years after, Lawrence Whistler's idyll of his love and marriage with Jill Furse, I seemed to recognize, in that record of the same years, the same quality of experience as had been mine; for what hair's breadth divides sacred from profane love, perfect realization like theirs from total illusion like mine! Moral or immoral, possible or impossible, the vision love pursues is everywhere and always the same, its source beyond any particular relationship that it may for the time illuminate.

I had not the fortitude to know myself alone. I find it possible, now, to write without turning, in imagination, to some beloved person; but that is because now I know that the only beloved is the living mystery itself. But then, my love was a dream I could not relinquish, for I could not live without the illusion that I was not alone; nor could I have endured the knowledge that I myself was the creator of those situations of unrequited love in which I suffered so much anguish. Yet so, I now understand, it was; my daimon chose for me the inaccessible. Useless to pity Sappho, or Emily Dickinson, or Christina Rossetti, for were not these too under the same compulsion to love only in situations which could not compromise essential solitude, an inner dedication so taken for granted it is not even perceived? I now see, as the type of every woman poet, that half-legendary poetess of Japan, Komachi, who, in her youth a court lady with many lovers, in her old age walked in rags on the roads of enlightenment.

It was not paradise, then, which failed or faded, but I myself who could not pass the test of offered beatitude. Sorrowful, reluctant, the guardians of my place of respite, peace and spiritual restoration, allowed me to sever the ties which bound me and to depart; go, being what I was, I must. I believe I was deeply wrong to go; for with my departure ended my children's brief time of freedom and happiness, their world woven among those fields and streams and magic places on the fell taken away from them, and all the hours and days of blackberrying and toast for tea by our own wood fire.

> . . . every Space that a Man views around his dwelling-
> place
> . . . such space is his Universe:
> And on its verge the Sun rises and sets, the Clouds bow.

In such a world we had lived; and leaving Martindale was like a mutilation;

> And if he move his dwelling-place his heavens also move,
> Where'er he goes, and all his neighbourhood bewail his
> loss . . .

It was Helen Sutherland's offer to take my children into her house in order to enable me to seek my fortune in London which made it possible for me to go. Yet I made a fatal mistake; I left my children too young and too soon; and Helen's standards of perfection, which from artists could call out the best, which from me had called out my best, for my children, I realized too late, would be an intolerable burden. I ought to have seen this all along, but I shut my eyes to signs I should have heeded, would have heeded, had I been less bent upon my own ends.

That autumn, day after golden day prolonged the summer. At last the appointed time of departure arrived, and I took my children to Cockley Moor. Only on our arrival did I see, with terrible clarity, what I should have seen before, that my children's freedom was over and Cockley Moor, to me a refuge, would be to them a prison. 'Go back,' my daimon said,' go back at once, it is not too late even now.' But how could I have explained to Helen, who towards me had been so full of forbearance and understanding, who in kindness had offered to help me? As so often when the daimon speaks, I answered that it was too late, impossible now, my plans made, other people involved, my course set. Ah, the wrong course, my daimon said; and I replied, 'what else can I do?' The daimon said nothing about how to earn a living. Yet the daimon is always right, and this the future always in time reveals. Even money I suppose would have been forthcoming if I had heeded more attentively the warning voices. I might then have been a better poet. I had, at Martindale, made a beginning, but nothing more; and had I followed up the poems of *Stone and Flower* with others—but it is useless now to guess what way my life might then have taken. Had I been offered my chance and proved unworthy of it? Or are such oases only places of respite, not of refuge? If I had, in those years of vision, relinquished carnal desire and the will o' the wisp 'love', might I have been allowed to remain? But that valley was my love; and my love, perhaps, that valley, woven into my dreams and fantasies, and my poems. And yet, someday, somehow, I would have had to go; I was in my early thirties, it was too soon to leave the world; what had seemed home proved to be only a stage in the journey. I remember William Empson quoting to me, on that walk by the lake-side to Patterdale,

> Does the road wind uphill all the way?
> Yes, to the very end.

We were both laughing, of course; I did not believe it. I have always been too ready to believe that the worst was over.

CHAPTER SEVEN

Orpheus in Hell

S T. TERESA was advised by her spiritual directors not to
follow her original intention of confessing, in her *Life*,
to her early sins; since from such an account no good
could come to her readers, whereas from her record of her
deepest insights others might learn. Everyone, after all,
knows the banalities of falling short, of our physicality,
ignorance and so forth. Modern practice has tended more
and more to reverse this view of what ought to be told and
what withheld. To lay bare base thoughts and actions is held
to be more 'sincere', and in this sense more truthful, than
to bear witness to those glimpses which come only at those
moments in which we seem to transcend our habitual
selves. The claim to have seen sublime or beautiful things,
because out of character with our commonplace selves, is
seen as a kind of hypocritical self-aggrandizement; even
though in fact it is only insofar as we all do transcend at
moments those vulgar selves that we can see or know anything of value. One might with no less reason call musicians
hypocrites who, mis-shapen shabby creatures, evoke from
wood and strings and metal and from their own bones and
sinews the music of the spheres. Or what truth can there
be in a 'sincere' and 'frank' wrong solution to a problem in
geometry? Only one solution is true, the rest are not other
truths about number, but failures to find it. In an age when
'the truth' is held to be a mere record of the flux of events,
truth itself is seen as a kind of untruth, because out of the
ordinary, above the ordinary. It was fashionable in my
youth to re-write the lives of poets, saints and others
remembered precisely insofar as they at certain moments

transcended their ordinary selves, in terms of a kind of mundane and animal realism; and this, it is implied is 'the truth' about Milton or Shelley or some other. Yet what such accounts omit is, precisely, the truth grasped by poet or saint in moments of insight, intuition of harmony and meaning, above the animality all share.

I have little, therefore, to tell of the shabby years following my return to London, since these were years of alienation from vision. There is yet another reason for my blanks in the record of this time: the difficulty of reviving the traces of memory. Freudians might say I have repressed things I do not want to remember because too painful or too humiliating; but my own belief is that I cannot remember because the events had so little reality in them: there is no inner content to remember. They were, like so much realistic fiction, uninteresting. Instead of memory there remains a symbol, my own dimly-lit and ill-constructed stage-set of the Hades where Orpheus, singing and playing his lyre (and if that music had ceased he would have been lost) wandering down deeper and deeper among the dead in his search for Eurydice.

The power of this symbol was strong in those war years; Kathleen Ferrier's voice singing *Orfeo*; the dream-like compulsion of Cocteau's Orphée that dark illusory caverned world (one remembers those sheets of glass, planes of illusion, not stable or fixed, but encountered here or there as they are carried for purposes unknown, by the glazier of windows) express the essence of something undergone by the imagination alienated from the light but not yet dead. In the pre-war days of Mass-Observation we had looked down, like Blake's 'eternals' about to fall into the abyss, on the sorrowful states below; but now I was myself treading paths unimaginably strange and desolate, no longer an 'observer', but travelling on foot, shelterless. I seemed again, after the sweet refuge of Martindale, to be walking on paths and ways not my own; but whether this was because the tidal wave of events had swept away all individual paths and ways, or because I had lost myself again, I do not know. If I

145

held on to my lyre it was less to play than to hold as a talisman; 'I am a poet,' I believed, 'and therefore the meaning of this experience must be found: for that I am here.'

I made the descent not, now, as a somnambulist but with a sense of quest; I felt it as a task imposed to explore these states, to endure that journey, to discover the limits of those distances. Perhaps it would not have been necessary for me to journey down there, from Martindale where I might have remained with my children, had not the darkness in myself drawn me into dark places; but better one's own nightmare than the shelter of someone else's dream; even our nightmares are expressions of our own reality, stations on our own way; and on that way it is always good to be.

From that shadow-world the images which return are all unconnected, for there was no form, no story. I cannot remember how I was directed, or by whom, to the furnished room in Percy Street to which I came. Years before, while I was still a schoolgirl, a fortune-teller had told me that I 'would always have a roof over my head'. This had seemed a strange promise, for I had not at that time doubted so ordinary a possibility. 'Honour thy father and thy mother, that thy days may be long in the land that the Lord giveth thee'; these words I had seen and read every morning when I woke in the blue bedroom at the Manse; but I had seen no necessary connection between my flight from my parents (whom I had not honoured) and the ways of the prodigal I now travelled. Now for the first—and by no means the last—time, that meagre promise of the Fates (the same fortune-teller had told me that although I would know true love I would not marry my love) seemed all I had to hold on to, so bottomless seemed the abyss at my feet. 'Time and the hour run through the roughest day' also brought me its arid comfort; but though like him I clung to oracles I lacked Macbeth's fortitude of desperation.

This room, then, was like a piece of wreckage to which I clung. So entirely alien was it, so unrelated to anything in my past, my future, my hopes or expectations, that I found myself invaded again by my old terror of loss of identity, of

146

foundering in the black flood of nonentity which poured like water into a sinking ship. My identity was still a most fragile paper-boat to which to entrust myself; I had become, again, one of the dispossessed, one of the multitude of 'displaced persons' caught up in the great torrent which has in this century swept so many human beings away from all securities, tearing up the roots of lives. I, who longed so much to be rooted for ever in the beloved place (and that place had for a while been Martindale) was by the compulsion both internal and external, torn away once more.

The house in question was let out in rooms to various young women working in war ministries. There is something sordid and vicious in the area of London west of Tottenham Court Road, which yet, like the seamier side of Balzac's Paris, exerts a powerful attraction upon a certain kind of *âmes damnées*: (phrases from Rimbaud and Baudelaire made our company of the damned into a kind of *élite*.) The finely proportioned early Georgian houses, running to dry-rot and decay, seemed to lend themselves, like rafts in a storm, to the struggle for survival, for a foothold in 'the world', which is, in those hells, so powerful a mirage; so near did the squalor of lonely back rooms rented by the month to lie to the White Tower and the Etoile, to all those favourite fashionable restaurants frequented by the ambitious engaged in using their talents in order to climb to the security of fame. These rooms were not places to be lived in, as the vicarage at Martindale was a place to be lived in (and even now that in retrospect I know what in prospect I did not know, how brief was to be my time there, Martindale seems to have been my home and my children's home for a period not measurable by time, so inexhaustible is it) but only to use as a base, a lair to hunt from and to take cover in. Solitude at Martindale was endlessly rich; but to have nowhere to go out to from those drab rooms, whose very furniture seemed displaced (there was a gate-legged oak table, I remember, to which I looked desperately for comfort and dignity, it and I alike having fallen from the good country world of a solid past) was to have the sense of
147

being banished from existence, with nothing to hold on to beyond a table and a chair and a gas-fire. In Martindale I had my own furniture which, however shabby, lent to me that sense of being mistress in my own house, without which few women can withstand adversity. The very hopes of such rooms as the one I now occupied are desperations, corks and straws tossing on the black gulfs; hope for some scrap of literary work (a book-review or the like) and hope for love, for love the saviour, the rescuer, the end of all sorrow; *Eldorado banal*, but we never think of that on our own *Voyage à Cythère*. And yet I had, of my own volition, exchanged Martindale for this .The world continually reflects back to us our inner states, and this was the aspect of mine. Had I but seen it for what it was; as perhaps in a sense I did, for I did give my inner assent to the experience, I was not, here as at Blackheath, oppressed by the despair of feeling myself passive in the power of others.

> My soul is like a ship in a dark storm
> Blowing I know not whither . . .

was a line which at that time haunted me; and Vittoria Corombona's kind of passion seemed reason enough for any storm and darkness. 'My sin was in my blood, and now my blood pays for't.' With pride, the last refuge of the damned, I made her words my own. Through what hells will we not walk undeterred, to destruction if need be, if passion drives us. In the overcoming of such a passion I could at that time see only a denial of life, and justified myself with Blake's 'those who overcome their desires do so because their desire is weak enough to be overcome'. 'If the fool will persist in his folly he will become wise' might have been more to the point, but I did not see myself as a fool. Webster's *flectere, si nequeo superos, Acheronta movebo* was more in my mood—Webster, who clothed crude and trivial lusts in the trappings of Renaissance splendour.

In the next room lived Sonia Brownell; and in that place of strangers she was the one person who welcomed me as someone whose name she already knew. But instantaneous recognition does not depend on hearsay; and in Sonia I recognized, in the Hades upon whose brink we met, another soul making a journey not unlike my own. Perhaps she would not have used at that time the words of the Order whose nuns had educated her, *magna est veritas*, but such was her faith. In pursuit of that unknown absolute, truth (for her a human truth higher at least than the positivist truth of Cambridge) she was prepared to venture all. Ulysses was her favourite hero because he was guided by intelligence. She always fell in love with intelligent men; and although constantly bedevilled by the current confusion of intelligence with cleverness, she was never long satisfied with the fashionable pseudo-answers the world she moved in offered her. In that world of worldly ambitions and wordly values she was (as my son when he began to read Stendhal said of her) *une âme noble et généreuse*, seeing in the despair into which she so often fell the price that must be paid by seekers after truth who would not be put off with easy answers. Nor was she wrong in regarding the French Existentialists (some of whom were to become later her closest friends) as the most intelligent seekers at that time in the Hades through which we moved.

Sonia may be said to have pursued that quest with more charity and fewer face-saving compromises than I. She has looked into the depths with eyes more merciful than mine, if perhaps a little too long.

Unlike myself Sonia had been educated within the framework of Catholic tradition which claims, by tried means, to attain assured ends. But she had rejected her Catholic, as I my Protestant framework, and for reasons in part similar: not from laxity, nor from want of a sense of final ends, but, because foregone conclusions appeared as arbitrary limits imposed upon possibility. Perhaps, since formulations of truth may themselves become opaque objects of idolatry, her rejection was of real falsifications, as mine had been; perhaps unfortunately for herself she retained from her early training in apologetics (years later she confessed to me, late one night, that she had come first in all England in apologetics in her last year at school) the habit of relying upon conceptual thinking in her search for final answers. In this she did constant violence to her own gift of deep and generous feeling, to which such thought often ran counter.

We were both alike under the influence of the spirit of the time, which equated the search for truth in every field (and in the arts especially) with the rejection of all truths of the past. Just because these had already been formulated they could not be that thing beyond, which art at all times seeks to embody. Eliot's insistence on tradition could not arrest the progressive dismantling of civilization (which indeed he himself saw) from the Impressionists to the Cubists, from the Surrealists to the Existentialists; which at that time still seemed exciting enough, a search for new, rather than what in truth it was, a progressive elimination of all possibilities. The writings of Herbert Read embody, in its most serious and responsible terms, what has proved yet another illusion, that the 'freeing' of the artist from tradition can lead to anything except the end of civilization as such. While Churchill conducted his war to save civilization from barbarism encroaching from without, the dismantling proceeded from within.

As with the arts we saw rules not as to be learned but to be broken, so in the conventions of morality we saw only a refusal to confront truthfully the issues of life; in life as in art we must find the answers for ourselves. It had not occurred to my generation that such answers take many thousands of years to find, nor, as Yeats had written, but in a book I had not then read, 'truth cannot be discovered, but may be revealed'. 'The way up is the way down' (T. S. Eliot had lent his authority to these words, written by a mystical theologian besides) is another of those statements which can only be misleading when taken out of context. The only context into which we incorporated any fragment we might discover had been created by ideologies themselves iconoclastic—Marxism, Freudian psychology, Surrealism; a whole within which no fragment of what in another context might be wisdom could keep its virtue. But we did not think the way down an easy way, or for that reason set out to explore the depths; on the contrary we took that journey, without certainty of way or end, as the harder and more heroic way. Conventional virtues seemed, by contrast, the effortless way, or rather a refusal to travel on the Way at all.

The one thing I had retained from my upbringing on the Romantic Poets and the Protestant religion was an absolute belief in the inner light of inspiration as the one sure guide. I found a text in the *Geeta* which says 'It is better to perish in one's own law; it is perilous to follow the law of another; better to fail in one's own way than to succeed in the way of another.' Again I seized upon the words out of context, and supposed the 'law' named the inner light; but the Hindu idea of *dharma* envisages social laws, laws of caste. To me, fugitive as I was from a social order I had never known from within, there was no social *dharma*, only the inner light; I lived as an outcaste. Yet I did believe that every life is a way; that we are given each our own clue to unwind, a clue to lead us through the labyrinth so long as we never lose it, never relinquish the living thread.

The obvious dangers of self-deception, the mistaking, for example, of carnal passion for the inner light (fuel upon which, nevertheless, as every poet has known, that light has often fed) never gave me pause. As for the end to which I might be led, I more than half knew that this could never be anything like marriage, nor even, when it came to the point, a real love affair. For the end to which my love pointed was some absolute beyond these. I cared only for pure love—using the term as one might distinguish between 'pure' and 'applied' mathematics. But, being weak and ignorant, I continued to delude myself for as long as I possibly could, and hoped, somehow, someday, for earthly happiness as well as the other goal.

Even now I cannot think I was mistaken in divining that we can be certain only of our love, must begin where that love is as the only ground on which we stand. If what we love be some Alastair, some mirage, even that mirage has a relative reality, the only reality which we are, at the moment

151

we perceive it, capable of perceiving. To extinguish or deny such love as we have is to be without any light whatsoever; for love, and not that denial of living impulse my father's generation so named, is will. 'Do what thou wilt is the whole of the law', as that lapsed Plymouth Brother, Frater Perdurabo wrote; I too was resolved to 'go through with it'. A difficult, austere and exacting law it proves to be, Crowley had said; and so I too was to find 'the unknown disciplines of the self-imposed task'. These (the phrase is Conrad's) I was to discover in due course.

What I did not know, or would not see, was how high a price others must pay for the way I took; my parents, my children. I see it now being paid still in the third generation, that of my grandchildren. If I had known this, would I have acted differently? I think not; we are all in the inextricable confusion, and grandchildren and great-grandchildren must bear their human burden like the rest. The answer may be, after all, an irreducible paradox; as David Lindsay states it in his strange symbolic book *A Voyage to Arctutus*. It is a woman drawn by music away from her family who in that book says 'I am conscious of two worlds. My husband and boys are real to me, and I love them fondly. But there is another world for me . . . and it makes my real world appear all false and vulgar.' 'But can it be right', the visitor from Earth asks her, 'to satisfy our self-nature at the expense of other people?' 'No, it is not right. It is wrong, and base . . . but in that other world these words have no meaning.' 'In place of a heart you have a wild harp, and that is all I know about you,' the earth-man says. Are heart and harp compatible? So I always hoped, but did not find it so.

People like myself are dangerous to social stability, since we have no loyalties native to us, but only those we ourselves choose; or none at all. And those we are likely to choose, once the simple ties of life are broken, are absolutes and perfectionisms. Social exiles are ruthless perfectionists; and if in the service of these absolutes we do not spare ourselves, neither do we understand compassion for the

152

limitations of others, or that these limits may be bounds set not so much to thwart life as to protect it and make it possible at all.

I believed myself a dedicated poet whose life was, if not a Christian pilgrimage, a legendary quest; but what was I, to the eyes of the world, but a young woman of no social background, who had left her husband, who had no visible means of support and wretchedly shabby clothes? Only my inner pride was equal to the many ordeals and humiliations which I at this time, and most deservedly, underwent. Through Janet I had been offered an obscure job in one of the many proliferating government departments created by the war; a department staffed by ladies of the diplomatic class, one of whom was an Oxford friend of Janet's. Among them I cut a wretched figure; not only because of my shabby and sordid exterior, but from my real ignorance of current affairs. I was, besides, unable to form any inkling of what kind of press-clippings constituted what were known as 'pointers', useful in a way I utterly failed to grasp, towards some end of propaganda or counter-propaganda which was equally dark to me. My clothes, my cough, my misery, my incompetence, my not belonging to their class and caste (and here indeed these women of the legislative or 'ruling' class were engaged in performing their traditional function, in their proper place and doing their proper work, whereas I was not) quickly earned me dismissal. I was passed on, somehow, to another but far more terrible department, connected with market-research, conducted this time by men of neither breeding nor education, where I was even more a misfit, and seemed back in the nightmare of Ilford, swallowed again into the gulf I most feared. What to the ladies of the Ministry, and to the men of the still lower depths, seemed real and important, seemed to me unreal and of no importance; and again I was oppressed by the number against me. Only alone did I still retain any secret refuges of beauty; in the outer world there seemed to be, for me, no place, no *terra firma*, and I found myself sinking and drowning and with no idea of which way to turn.

153

At Christmas I fled north to Helen Sutherland, to see my children; strangely removed from me they seemed, under her care, our family relationship no longer unbroken. But we went, for a few days, (Helen must have paid for us) to the Howtown Hotel, just over the familiar hill from Martindale; in sight still, but already for ever out of reach. There, snowed up, behind great wind-carved sculptured drifts of snow we were safe from the world for a little while. It was a sweet secret time, shut off from all that lay outside and beyond; and then it was over, and I returned to London with, again, no job and no income. I remember waiting for the night train on blacked-out Carlisle station; waiting interminably in one of those non-places that war seemed to create; filled with people who were, like myself, walking in that grey cold dream. Sitting beside me on a seat on the platform was a young Scotswoman, certainly much younger than I was myself, who might once have been pretty; but now all her hair had fallen out, from some loathsome disease, and she stank; she had no idea of how she was going to reach her destination in London—if she had one—where she was travelling, following up some desperate thread she hoped would lead her to some man or other to whom she was or was not married, but bound by sorrow; she herself hardly expected to find him, but the need to search drove her. 'I was a silly lassie' she said, judging herself more mercifully than I (of whom she seemed a terrible caricature) could judge myself. There is something in that word, 'lassie' (a word my mother had so often used of me and to me) that absolves from all blame, so innocent, so fresh and fair and vulnerable is the young form it evokes. It is a word of endearment; not especially a lover's endearment but the ambient endearment of family love, of village (for it is a folk-word), of a whole environment of belonging. I wished that there was now anyone to use that word of me, and a great nostalgia for that past world from which some dark dirty train was about to carry me away weakened my courage. I gave the poor ruined creature what money I could—very little: a gesture of self-pity.

154

As for 'the literary world' I had set out to find and conquer, I found myself ill-equipped for the task. I was too proud to serve and too ignorant and inexperienced to be, for example, the literary editor of a weekly newspaper. Sonia, secretary and general assistant on the literary magazine *Horizon* introduced me to Cryil Connolly and Peter Watson. Cyril Connolly once or twice published articles of mine in *Horizon* (none of any merit) and a poem or two; indeed (perhaps for Sonia's sake) he reviewed my first volume of poems with discernment (as it seemed to me, since he praised the poems). But our values were not the same and yet I could not see that, this being so, I could not hope to succeed in the literary *haut monde*. I suffered from a twofold ignorance: of my own strength, as a poet, had I more courageously entrusted myself to it; and of my own limitations. Those who are without a certain range of knowledge or sensibility may be vaguely aware of a lack, but can never form a clear or just estimate of that in which we fall short; because in order to form that just estimate we should have to possess the very knowledge we lack. Thus the uneducated classes see those above them only in terms of such values as they themselves possess; and I still did not possess (my Cambridge years notwithstanding) either the intangible standards, or the exact knowledge, of the élite to which I half aspired. I was still at that time unable to assess those limitations in myself those not in these respects as ignorant as myself could see at a glance. 'Until you have knowledge of a man's ignorance, hold yourself ignorant of his knowledge,' Coleridge wrote; a warning flouted by every rising avant-garde. Such standards as those by which I measured myself then, and by which I was weighed and found wanting, have since all but disappeared; the barbarians now so vastly outnumber people of culture that they themselves now set the standards; with the resulting decadence in every field of art and learning of which it is unnecessary to say more, since it is self-evident to those who are not themselves examples of it, and impossible to grasp by those who are.

I was sure only when I was alone; I wished neither to follow any current fashion, nor to go against; only to write poetry which might reflect some gleam of a beauty of whose vision no one could rob me. I had met most of the writers of my own generation, and many others, yet I remained essentially a solitary, uncommitted. But I wished, at that time, for a word of praise from T. S. Eliot more, I think, than I have ever wished for praise before or since. He had published Charles's poems, and Michael's, and those of other friends and acquaintances; and before I left Martindale I had sent him the manuscript of my first collection of poems; but he returned it. Wait, he said, another two or three years. He may have been right; yet I think he was not looking for such qualities as my poems may have had, but for others which they did not possess. I do not remember how many years later it was that, at a dinner-party, he admitted he had had afterthoughts; though only tacitly, for what he said was, '*Another* mistake I made was over David Gascoyne.' (It was indeed.) I do not think he could ever have really liked my poetry, or David Gascoyne's; Edwin Muir was another poet whose work he only slowly came to think well of. We were all alike seeking to express a vision other than his own powerful and potent verse communicated.

Failing to find immediate acceptance in the literary world, or to receive the benediction of the greatest man of letters, I found a true friend of my poetry in Tambimuttu, editor of *Poetry London*. Kafka's Herr K., instructed in advance on how to know by their dress messengers from the Castle, nonetheless unaccountably disregarded the signs because the bearers of them were not the kind of people he had expected, nor did they come in the way he had anticipated. So it was with Tambi; for if many presentable figures in the literary world were shams, Tambi was a rajah in beggar's rags. If for the former, literature was not an end but a means (to wealth, to the pleasure of being famous, and to many more ephemeral vanities and advantages), for Tambi, poetry was the end to which mere wealth, worldly position or power were at best a means. The true aristocrat, St. John Perse's 'free man of

156

high caste', who possesses as by natural right all that the competitive world struggles for, is alone free to renounce all these for intangibles. So it was with Tambi, who valued immaterial above material riches, even though he did not practise the austerities of Prince Siddartha. His bohemianism was extreme, and alarming in its excesses to English eyes unused to so truly Oriental a contempt for even minimal securities. Tambi would have slept, and for all I know did sleep, on the pavements of London without a thought of discomfort, and without loss of some essential dignity. He lived in some squalid room (though sleep seemed to be something he never needed) his clothes were dirty and torn, his fingers, flexible and expressive as those of a dancing Shiva, stained with nicotine; money, when he had it, he spent or gave away with lavish generosity to unworthy recipients overnight without, however, regretting or even remembering it, the next day.

As I was swept along by the turbid river into which I had fallen, it was Tambi who pulled me ashore. I had met him at some time in the past, I suppose; I believe he had come to visit Charles at Blackheath. Now on the pavement of Aldwych Tambi suddenly materialized, like an *avatar* of dancing Shiva, and greeted me, not as a former acquaintance, but as an eternal acquaintance. In such recognitions there is no dissimulation, no possible deception; no ulterior motives are involved. Tambi in his descent into bohemia (and no one ever descended lower and his beautiful features were often disfigured with the scars of drunken fights, usually in the cause of poetry) never lost the power of immediate divination of qualities. He had the gift of instantly recognizing the *rasa* (he himself used that Indian word) of whatever belongs to the imagination.

There may be works of great talent which are nevertheless on a lower plane of intellectuality than seemingly slighter works of imagination. Cyril Connolly recognized talent with as sure an instinct as Tambi recognized imagination; and, naturally enough, had more thanks for it, both from the producers and the consumers of literature. But Tambi knew all the poets, from T. S. Eliot downwards, who had any spark of eternity in them. 'He is really a wild man like me,' he used to say of Mr. Eliot, whom he loved, making a *mudra* with his nicotine-stained fingers; and Mr. Eliot, whose expressions of friendship were most guarded, used to claim to be the only person able correctly to pronounce a Tamil name: 'Not Tambi, *Thumbi.*'

Tambi, then, drew me to land as simply as a fisherman pulls a fish out of the water. I did not particularly want to be landed by Tambi, feeling it beneath my dignity; and I was not as grateful as I should have been. I took it as my due (which it may have been, but why then had I so wanted to be praised by T. S. Eliot or the editor of *Horizon*?) that he said to me repeatedly (like the applause, *baku, baku* of the enraptured auditors of Indian music) 'Kathleen, you are a *great poet*, I will publish your poems, it will be a beautiful book, you will see—' I did not more than half care; Eliot's rejection had wounded my pride more than Tambi's praise could flatter it. I was, besides, too completely possessed by the passion which drove me through fiery hells, walking on knives after the mirage of love, to care very much for the reality which was, after all, the poetry. Yet at the same time a part of me knew very well that my poetry, and Tambi's praise of it, were a reality, and all that walking on knives, all that anguish, relatively unimportant. Even so, I did not really care; to be rejected by the great and 'discovered' by Tambi I felt to be humiliating rather than flattering; and to my beautiful beloved, my poems had no existence at all. Besides all this, I did not feel that any of the poems I had as yet written were the poems I was capable of writing, and which at that time I still hoped and believed I would someday write.

But Tambi believed both in the poetry I had written, and in the poetry I would write; he believed in me as a poet with unconditional certainty; and my first volume, *Stone and Flower*, together with David Gascoyne's *Poems 1937–42* were published with the *Poetry London* imprint. Both volumes were beautiful, especially David's with its sombre illustrations by

Graham Sutherland that so perfectly suited the poems. My own *Stone and Flower* was illustrated by Barbara Hepworth. I had learned to admire, in Helen's house, the perfect taste of Ben Nicholson's abstract forms, discerning in them the kind of detached clarity of mind to which I had myself aspired during an earlier phase, as a student of biology, and again at the time of Mass-Observation. It was Ben who suggested that Barbara should illustrate my poems, from some notion about a woman's painting going with a woman's poetry. If there was an affinity between Barbara Hepworth and myself, it was not I think by reason of our sex, but much more of our period. It seemed to me at the time that what we had in common was a sense of the interior landscape of contemporary science; and so perhaps we had, though it is hardly apparent in my poems. In her work I found the same cool cold quality as in Ben's, the same 'detachment'. Oliver Simon of the Curwen Press printed both David's book and mine. He too cared for poetry for its own sake, and cared enough for mine to introduce me, when *Poetry London* collapsed, to my second publisher, Hamish Hamilton, for whom he designed my second book.

At a time when the fashion was for political writing or for wit, Tambi discerned and valued only imaginative vision. He made remarkably few mistakes, for fashion never distracted him: yet I often wondered how he knew a good poem from a bad, for he never seemed to read them. Typescripts would lie about on his table, for months sometimes, and after a time he would pull one out and say 'This is a *great poem*'; and he would be (allowing for superlatives) right; a poem it would be. The rest he just left to accumulate to mature or fade as the case might be. He never returned these faded manuscripts, which were, for him, simply blank pages. He only noticed, by some kind of supra-sensible radiance they possessed, poems which had imaginative essence. And *Poetry London* made literary history for a while; its Lyrebird covers by Moore, Sutherland, Craxton, Ceri Richards, Cecil Collins, Gerald Wilde, are period pieces.

159

Tambi attempted books in which painter and poet collaborated, and did produce several most beautiful volumes, including my own. That they were uneconomic was, for him, neither here nor there.

Tambi even gave me a niche, for a while, in the *Poetry London* office; which itself was a niche within the offices of the publishers Nicholson and Watson. My duties were indeterminate; but it was a refuge from the terrifying limbo into which I had fallen.

Tambi used to tell me that his uncle was the greatest aesthetician of the century. I did not believe him; but it was true. I had not then read Coomaraswamy's works which, years later, I discovered to contain almost everything I have myself since come to believe about the arts. Coomaraswamy might have deplored the attraction by which Tambi was drawn from Ceylon to London's bohemia; but Tambi, instinctively, looked in poetry for those qualities which were, as Coomaraswamy saw it, its essence: 'Art is expression informed by ideal beauty.' In positivist Cambridge the old notion that some ideas were in themselves of more value as coming from a 'higher' source, than others, had been dismissed. Again with Tambi, and later in my reading of his illustrious uncle's works, I found Dante's truth proclaimed: poetry was not merely to state true things beautifully, but 'beautiful things truly'.

Visiting New York in 1962 I found Tambi living, as usual, in a slum street of peculiar grimness. I made my way there, at dusk, in some fear, for the taxi-driver had deposited me at the wrong address, several blocks away, outside a bar that seemed to be also both a laundry and a brothel or thieves' kitchen; and I made my way on foot, keeping to the middle of the street to avoid the sinister groups on the pavement. Not finding Tambi's name on any door or board, I asked a tiny beautiful star-like dark girl, an Italian probably, if she would take me to her mother so that I could ask; but half-way up the sinister stairs we met three girls who might have come from the film *West Side Story*; the gentleman with long hair? they said; and from their warmth I gathered that here

160

too Tambi inspired affection. Yes, he lived in the basement. So I made my way down among the dustbins and the electric meters (the stucco, though decayed, was beautiful, and that too was characteristic of Tambi) but when the door opened, there was Tambi wearing an Indian dress of spotless white. His young wife was expecting a baby (my god-daughter) the room had been distempered, and the varnish on the floor was scarcely dry. In my honour Tambi and the son of the former financial supporter of *Poetry London* (Richard March) had worked day and night to finish it. Billy March, on leaving Bryanston, had crossed the Atlantic to be with Tambi, because he had loved him as a child; his own father being dead, he now called Tambi father.

Not only had he splendidly scraped and distempered the walls, but had taken upon his young shoulders the responsibility of Tambi's precarious household. The furniture had been provided by Tambi's cousin, Coomaraswamy's daughter Rohini, the 'cellist. Even her Brahmin pride and family disapproval had somehow melted into affection before the innocence of bohemianism as extreme as Tambi's to which disapproval seemed no longer applicable, as a curve becomes a straight line at infinity. So some of Coomaraswamy's furniture and fine silk curtains found their way, like other more intangible inheritances, into Tambi's underworld; if underworld it can be called, where so many essential values were preserved.

Tambi's younger brother Augustin, a Jesuit, tried to show him the error of his ways from time to time, and even visited New York in order to do so. I hope he too was disarmed; as I was myself on receiving, in 1967, a letter from Tambi, now the 'guru' in charge of Timothy Leary's 'ashram' in Upper New York State; he offered me honorary membership, adding 'you need not take drugs if you're squeamish.' How trivial my moral disapproval beside Tambi's loyalty!

Among the faces that emerge from the shadows of war-time London David Gascoyne's remains memorable; for he, too, coming, I suppose, into the *Poetry London* office (for I have no memory of place in which to situate my memory of his

161

person) greeted me, as had Tambi, not as an old acquaintance or as a new one, but as an eternal companion met down there in Hades. I remember well how beautiful he was when, before the war, he used to visit Charles and Humphrey at Blackheath, how gentle and defenceless, but, like a wild animal who has never yet had cause to fear man, open and expectant only of receiving the same goodness and outflowing love that was in him. His fine poet's eyes were full of sensibility and nobility, his eloquent mouth vulnerable; a child of Paradise cast upon our world. Life had not yet hurt him, and he was happy in his early recognition as a poet. He was intoxicated by Surrealism at that time, and he and Humphrey were both active in the Surrealist exhibition. (David I seem to remember escorted in Trafalgar Square a girl whose head was entirely encased in a mask of roses.) He also wrote *A Short History of Surrealism*, since republished. Now meeting him again (he had been living in Paris until the outbreak of war) in war-time London I was shocked by the change in him; for now he looked racked, tormented, his large hands forever moving nervously, twisting a handkerchief, his deer-like eyes haunted; his teeth were decayed, his skin grey. He still had no mask or defensive barricade, and he still had the same sweetness; and where he sensed sympathy he assumed in others a truth of feeling equal to his own. He had now a new volume of poems (*Poems 1937–1942*) ready for publication. Now that these poems have outlived the moment that produced them, the greatness of some of them apparent to all who care for poetry, I wonder at the miracle by which a sensitivity so vulnerable as his survived and found eloquence in a world so ruinous.

Later, when I was living precariously at 9 Paulton's Square, by all manner of literary hack-work, translations, reviewing and so on (all made infinitely more difficult than it need have been by the interior condition of anguish against which I laboured) David took refuge with me for a while. He was, at that time, even more ill than he had been at the time of *Poetry London*. He used to say that it was as if his 'brain leaked'; (he later described it as 'like a transistor set inside his head', on which all kinds of voices not his own spoke, wept, declaimed, argued, chanted; while others would say 'we are the gods, the gods'). But he read continuously, widely and deeply in works of mystical philosophy, and existentialism, and talked, rapidly and eloquently, of the divine vision which haunted his darkness like the sun at midnight—an image he himself used—of Boehme, Hölderlin, Kierkegaard, Chestov, all the dark visionaries. He was writing, then, the poems of *A Vagrant* and *Night Thoughts*, and had, besides, a manuscript (never published and now lost) of *pensées* from the philosophers he read. He would lie for hours face downwards on his bed, or wander long in solitary night-walks. To me he turned as a fellow-poet whom he could trust absolutely; trust, for example, not to make emotional demands on him.

Other friends, concerned for the mortal man more perhaps than I was and less for the poet, were eager to put him in the hands of the psychiatrists; but a lyre so finely strung as David Gascoyne's imaginative sensitivity to the invisible currents was not for grosser hands to finger. Although he was, in his natural self, defenceless, to say the least, he had the poet's instinct to protect the lyre. He actually went, one day, to the Tavistock clinic, where, after an interview, the Freudian who saw him said, 'I am afraid I can do nothing for you'; David (his sense of irony was extremely subtle, and played often over his dark landscape) replied, 'then perhaps you will pray for me?' The psychiatrist very stiffly responded, 'I am afraid I do not believe in prayer!' David returned to tell the story which we both thought extremely funny, though (for the Freudian) also sad, and, of course, terrifying, when one recalls that in such hands are the souls of so many. For the rest, the proud Orphic lyre-bearer in him accepted the humiliations of the natural man the daimon so precariously inhabited. It is characteristic of him that he did not fear to speak of God to a professional unbeliever, for he never doubted that in everyone there is the divine light.

Other faces emerged and vanished in that phantasmagoria.

Louis MacNeice I did not know very well (indeed I passed as a stranger through those years) but he occasionally took me out to dinner, and gave me odds and ends of writing to do for the BBC; which I did with extreme labour and difficulty, as I did everything except the writing of poetry. Louis was most kind to my struggling and largely worthless efforts. I remember sitting in his company one evening, in the Café Royal probably, and his making up a half-serious fantasy about people who either had, or did not have, 'a little candle' alight in them. He himself still shone, in those days, with a poet's soft interior light which one might imagine coming from the rath of the *Sidhe*. This fine Irish poet, 'baptized with fairy water', was at that time in 'A.R.P.', and he once described to me how he had, the night before, been shovelling incendiary bombs off the dome of St. Paul's. I saw less of Louis with the years; but the last time was only a few weeks before his death, at a publisher's party given for the American poet Robert Lowell. There were many faces from the past; William Empson was there, and Ivor and Dorothea Richards, and Sonia and Cryil Connolly, and many to whom I could not even give names any more; like figures depicted in some Italian painting, all portraits of faces once known. Louis was there, grey now, but still with something of his former poet's look. To my surprise and pleasure and shame both he, whom I had not seen for years, and William Empson, from whose ways of thought, brilliant but perverse as it has come to seem to me, I had for long been, little by little, dissociating myself, greeted me with the kiss of friendship. Can we resemble Judas in the receiving, as in the giving, of a kiss? I felt this especially in relation to William; who had as good reason, after all, to dissociate himself from me; but it is not in his nature to be disloyal to any once a friend. So I found when an essay I had published on Blake's poems *A Little Girl Lost* and *Found* came under attack by some New Critic, and William rushed (in print) to my defence; as did Sir Geoffrey Keynes, but that was on Blake's behalf, whereas William's defence was on mine. At that same party Sonia whispered aside to me, 'But none of them

164

look in the least like poets!' I pointed out that very few of them wrote like poets either, and that the few who did, looked like poets: William, Louis MacNeice, Robert Lowell, himself, Ivor Richards (wizard of poetry if not quite poet), all these had memorable faces indeed. I have never found that people's looks belie them; David Gascoyne, Edwin Muir, Vernon Watkins, all those who have a daimon have a certain listening look. T. S. Eliot, for all his guarded austerity, had it; and from the eyes of Alexis Léger the diplomat looks St. John Perse the poet; eyes enchanted by 'les merveilles' which fill his world. (La terre enfante des merveilles, he wrote in Anabase.)

Michael Roberts presently came down to London to the European Service of the BBC, and his presence, more than anyone's, gave me a sense of continuing identity; for Janet and Michael were friends not only of the poet but of the poor human creature I was. Michael was always protective towards me, realizing how helplessly lost I was. William Empson, too, broadcasting programmes to the Far East, seemed to think that a poem or two of mine, recorded and transmitted, could help the war-effort; or perhaps that from the waste of effort involved in the war he might retrieve a poem or two. Like all Wykehamists I have ever known (even more than most) William had the gift of resuming anywhere, under any circumstances, in a squalid room in Marchmont Street, in a BBC Canteen, or in a Chinese holy mountain I do not doubt, or in smoking hell itself, a relationship, like an interrupted conversation, exactly where it had last been broken off. But I, unsure of myself, over-sensitive to mental climates and atmospheres created by others, had not that gift of creating everywhere the norm to which any surroundings become peripheral, and became flooded and possessed and overwhelemed by surroundings, from which I suffered unendurably, and from whose overwhelming I could escape only by flight; and I could not always fly. Only alone could I return to my own norm, my interior sanctuary. Alone, some indestructible supernatural strength of imagination sustained me.

Alone I could still swing back, like a compass-needle released by other magnets, to my own centre. Never, therefore, so much as in those London years, was I so grateful to the few friends who never deserted me for the assurance their continued existence gave me of my own; for I had no room of my own now, no white house in its garden with coal-tits in the yew-tree, no burn fringed with birch and alder to walk beside where I could listen to my own daimon and to the elemental voices.

Humphrey Jennings too reappeared in London; Cicely, with their two daughters, was in New York, and Humphrey had a room over the Etoile restaurant. That was like Humphrey, who loved good French cooking; in a French, practical way he settled into the best restaurant in Charlotte Street *en pension*. He was making war documentary films, of which *Fires Were Started*, a film about the London fire service, remains one of the few of the innumerable contemporary works about the working-class which sincerely and convincingly depicts 'the people' in terms of heroic Churchillian glory, without sentimentality and without vulgarity. Such films had been made in Russia, but nothing comparable in England. Humphrey after the war said that it was a sad truth that only the situations of war could give to the common people opportunities to show their finest innate qualities. The war, or perhaps Churchill's eloquence, called to the soul of Albion for the last time, and in those years all kinds of people (the fat red-haired woman who went back to serving vegetables in the greengrocer's, the sweep who lost a finger and won a George Medal rescuing people trapped in a bombed building at the World's End) showed their worth who afterwards merged again into some meaningless background. Humphrey had been closer to Charles and to Mass-Observation than I had ever been, and his war-films were perhaps the fruit of the imaginative moment they had shared and created.

Humphrey was still carrying about with him in a portfolio *Pandemonium*, his never-completed anthology of the Industrial Revolution, pulling out one page or another descriptive of

166

the impact on the old eighteenth-century pastoral England of the Dark Satanic Mills, declaiming it to such friends as emerged to vanish again into the blackout of our own war-time pandemonium, illuminated by flames not unrelated to Milton's pitch and nitre; for the Royal Society had started the whole terrible process (such was the theme of Humphrey's book) the Mills of Satan appearing first, as Blake had long ago declared, in the mechanistic theorizings of Bacon, Newton and Locke; only later to be reflected in those machines, their expression and image, from whose relentless wheels it seems our world can no longer (whether in peace or in war) extricate itself. Humphrey's anthology was at once an indictment, a lamentation, and a glorification of a race and a nation. For up to the end of the war, for all the multiplication of the dispossessed who have no memory, and who have therefore lost the threads of tradition with which a nation is woven through time, England was still an imaginative as well as an economic entity. Like Churchill, Humphrey saw England's present glory in the light of her past, of Pitt and Nelson, of Stubbs and Gainsborough, of Blake and Gray and Inigo Jones. He himself gave in his war films a last expression of a civilization specifically English. Now the English language has become the *lingua franca* of world barbarism and the landmarks of the past are fast disappearing. I remember walking with Humphrey among the wreckage of houses, where rain dripped down from charred beams and wallpaper hung in tatters, through Blake's Golden Square and the streets of Soho, Humphrey all the time talking of Blake, so that we seemed to be walking within those very blood-vessels of the city to which Blake had likened 'London's darkening streets'.

At the time of Churchill's State funeral I stood my three night hours with the long procession of that English nation, reassembled for the last time; moving—as the cutting East wind blew up the Thames from the docks and warehouses where Humphrey had made his heroic film of the London blitz, from Greenwhich where with him, in the imaginative enchantment of Mass-Observation days, I had so often

walked from the Trafalgar Tavern to the Woolwich tunnel
—a few steps at a time from Blake's Lambeth across London's
river, and so to Westminster Hall. It was of Humphrey I
thought, and of Michael Roberts, who on V-day had come
to Chelsea and sought me out, to walk on the embankment
and drink in the Black Lion, sharing for once a collective
emotion. Our own wartime past seemed to belong to a
present continuous with the cold waters of the Thames as
they reflected that night the lights of the city, the old
dolphin lamp-posts, the glowing face of Big Ben, silent that
Friday midnight when I stood with the anonymous English
nation, awakened, perhaps for the last time, to a collective
imaginative sense of the continuity and glory of the history
of its great city.

After the war I saw Humphrey less often; he would reappear, from time to time, and always with some glory of
the world to tell of; but not, any more, of England; he had
turned his back upon the industrial modern world, the
tragic infernal greatness of Pandemonium; quite lost faith
in, and turned away from, the modern West. Once he had
just returned from Greece (where he was making a film)
and spoke of the life of shepherds and goatherds in the
barren hills; the life of Arcadia itself, still to be found in the
simplicity of a kind and quality of poverty which in no way
destroyed the dignity of illiterate men with half-wild dogs
to guard their flocks, women whose houses were beautiful
by the very absence of the trash of the machines, 'functional'
because in them were only such things as body and soul
require: hearth, woollen or goat's hair blankets woven on a
loom; figs drying in the sun; a vine with grapes, great loaves
of bread baked in an oven built of clay, milk and honey and
bread and wine. He did not speak of the continued spiritu-
ality of Orthodox Christianity and was, I think, still dreaming of a Socialist Utopia without the machine; a classless
anarchy. But, most and last, he was moved by Burma, where
he found the human society which to him seemed to come
nearest to an ideal perfection: a traditional Buddhist society,
where all took its meaning from its orientation towards a

spiritual vision. All, as he explained, from the weaving of the basket in which men carried their vegetables to market, to the burial of the dead, was done according to that philosophy which holds in a single thought the impermanence of all things and the existential mystery of the here and now. Years before he had talked of Lao-Tze; and now he had found a society which cared nothing for the permanence of things made, because the *tao* is inexhaustible: 'work it, and more comes out'. He had been present at the cremation of a Buddhist monk, and had, perhaps for the only time in his life, there understood what it is when an entire society is informed by a sublime metaphysical vision; something lost, or all but lost, from the modern West.

But Humphrey's solar hair was white; and my last memory of him is walking across the river from Paulton's Square to visit Battersea Old Church, where Blake had married his Catherine; standing, still, an intelligible though modest expression of classic proportion on its little peninsula of Thames mud where working-class children play. Upstream, the landscape of nineteenth-century industry, trucks clanking across a railway-bridge, beyond the smoking chimneys of Lot's Road power-station; downstream, London, its old aspect already changing before the encroachment of office-blocks, inhuman and anonymous. Half-way across Battersea bridge Humphrey paused and raised his arm in the old eighteenth-century orator's gesture; and the Thames, before that gesture (which embraced Dryden's *King Arthur*, the *Triumphs* of Gray and the *Masks* of Inigo Jones, the declamations of Los and the stance of Gainsborough's slender and elegant country gentlemen) became again Spenser's Sweet Thames, now the 'chartered Thames' for so long that its defilement and servitude had become irrevocable. And yet, Humphrey said, in that river, free from pollution, fish might breed again, silver salmon to feed the people of London. All kinds of living silvery shoals once came there; and as he spoke the muddy foul waters flowing under us towards the Tower Bridge, Greenwich, and the docks where Humphrey had made his *Fires Were Started*,

169

became transformed by Humphrey's inimitable magic into Blake's 'spiritual fourfold London'. The royal swans at least were still there, no less numerous or less beautiful than when Sir Thomas More's gardens ran down to the river at the very place we stood; they were feeding, now, on the waste from the Hovis flour-mills (only a little up-stream from the site of Blake's Albion flour-mill) below the Morgan crucible-works; another dark satanic heritage of the triumph of the material interests of industry over the aesthetic idealism of the pre-Raphaelite potter William de Morgan, whose beautiful ceramics could still be seen exhibited in Battersea Old House, and occasionally bought in the antique shops of the King's Road, birds and flowers and Morris willow-leaves in peacock and Persian blues and greens. That was the last of many walks with Humphrey through the streets of London which, in his company, always entered another dimension and became 'ideas of imagination'; as in former days his vision could translate the white wooden palings of Newmarket back into Stubbs' century, or the elms of North Essex into a landscape in China, the tangibility of Constable dissolving at his will into the void which upholds the ten thousand creatures. It seems in retrospect like the valediction of Blake's Los over London's vanished glory. Not long after Humphrey was killed, accidentally falling from a cliff on the island of Poros fatally injuring his head on the rocks below. He is buried in Greece, the country in which he had found 'the good life'.

I did not know of Humphrey's death at the time; but I had a dream on the night he died; the first occasion on which I was certain that some telepathic communication had reached me from the dead. The symbolic dress of such dreams is no doubt given by the dreamer; but the content surely not. This dream was coloured by deep, awe-inspiring emotion. I was in a Gothic cathedral, an immense stone building in which were many sculptured tombs and chantry-chapels. I looked long at the effigies, in stone, of three 'weepers' on a tomb, a woman and her two young daughters (Humphrey did leave a wife and two daughters

170

to mourn him) and as I looked the words 'a rocky death, a rocky death' were repeated, over and over. I then found myself in a chantry-chapel (and were not such shrines devoted to prayers for the dead?) and a voice which I did not recognize, but which I have since believed was Humphrey's, spoke to me of death in a way that brought to my consciousness the very experience of the reality of having to relinquish this life. 'However long you may stay in the sanctuary that protects you now', I was told, 'remember that sooner or later you will have to leave it.' The voice itself was serene, and it was I who trembled because death lay before me, not, as for the happy dead, behind: the 'sanctuary' I knew to be this life, in which I was hiding. The symbol of my dream was one of those small beautiful sixteenth-century chantry-chapels to be seen in the cathedrals of the south of England (in Winchester, for example) but to me the emotion associated with the 'sanctuary' comes from the lion's-head knocker of Durham Cathedral. Now I was made to understand the slightness and impermanence of that shelter; and I was filled with sorrow for myself, and a sort of envy for the speaker, for whom death was not a terror before, but an ordeal already over-passed. And was I, in my low and narrow stone sanctuary, or was the mysterious speaker, among the dead? As the voice ceased I heard the singing of a great choir, and, my voice choked with weeping, I tried to join in the singing—the Gloria of Bach's B-minor Mass. As the voices of the host of heaven and earth rose, the mourners below seemed to be uplifted out of grief on the music of the solemn four-note ascending phrases, carried upward and out of the stone cathedral and into an angelic world of light. Whereupon I awoke. Until I came to write this account I had not remembered that 'angels singing' was, among my father's people, often heard at the time of a death and understood as an omen of death; music being the form under which the human imagination clothes our perception of a sublime harmony. Only two or three days later did I learn of Humphrey's death.

171

CHAPTER EIGHT

Doors of Sanctuary

JUST AS Martindale vicarage seemed given rather than found, so did 9 Paulton's Square, which for many years to come was to be my home. It was through Helen Sutherland I came there, and in my worst hour. Returning to London houseless, without any job or source of income, I went, at her suggestion, to her friend Constance (Cooie) Lane, an artist, who also let rooms in her house to friends, and friends of friends. I do not recollect what time of year it was, but my impression is as of spring, early March, perhaps; of sitting in the back of the double room on the ground-floor—then Cooie's studio—with the sun filtering through the branches of the pear-tree in the garden behind. We sat by a little fire we could scarcely see for sunlight, and I poured out to Cooie Lane my troubles; she listened, and took me in, and that night I slept in a room that seemed fresh with the freshness of the trees outside my windows. There were some of Cooie's paintings on the walls—one was of petunias growing in plant-pots on some little balcony in France, or maybe in Italy; some quiet sweet place. All was plain, perhaps even shabby, though it did not seem so, but rather had the air of a house whose chairs and curtains and tables and plants were inhabitants, a group of old friends, well-born but poor. Years later I visited the small Franciscan monastery in Fiesole; there were pots of aspidistra, double daisies in the little formal flower-beds in the cloister, and singing birds, which so vividly recalled to me not so much the outward as the inner aspect of Cooie Lane's house that it was almost hallucinatory. Perhaps it was because in both (though her house was not otherwise obviously like a

172

cloister) all that chanced to come were taken in; and however long or short the time of sojourn of flower-pot, or lodger, or faded linen chair-cover, all were accepted; not necessarily liked (and that too might happen within the cloister) but the disliked person or thing would no more have been banished than creatures from the creation. 'Let all grow together until the harvest' was one of her many sayings. That, perhaps, even more than her artist's poverty, is what Cooie's house had about it that St. Francis' monastery recalled; and, again like a monastery, there was a sense of leisure, of time there being free. Partly it may have been also something Italian in her taste; her Arundel prints, the pieces of green silk, the Florentine pottery and the garden vine. To wake in the cleanness of that room was like waking, healed, after a long illness. I woke there, for the first time since I had left Martindale, with the sense of being once more in my right place and not in a nightmare. Later the house was to become mine; and much of her old furniture, her pear-tree and her vine; yet I could not keep her atmosphere. Her house was what it was because all of a piece, its values, its people, down to its chipped pots and patched linen; what I made never had the Franciscan beauty of what she had made; no parasite can inherit the bee's knowledge or the secret of its honey.

Cooie suffered from a serious heart-disease and one night, soon after my arrival, she had an attack, and I sat up all night with her, comforting her, and holding her hands. I think that was why she gave me her friendship, afterwards, so fully. I tried, certainly, to help her—I could have done no less—and she turned to me as an ally and protector. She talked to me by the hour in her cracked but beautiful contralto voice, with gestures of her dry tapered Holbein fingers. She was full of humour, and a wonderful mimic, especially of cockney; and her characteristic word of advice —she gave it to me but I disregarded it, so diametrically opposite was it to my own natural bent—was *le mieux est l'ennemi du bien.* An old maid herself, she perhaps felt that romantic love had been a will o' the wisp; or perhaps she

173

was trying to tell me (or herself) that her house and its chipped Italian cups and her crayons and work-table was *le bien*, if not Helen Sutherland's 'the best *is* the best'. *Le mieux* for Cooie, was not only rich relations, lords and ladies and lovely cousins who had made distinguished marriages, lived in great houses, had beautiful children; it was also artists more successful than herself—Ben Nicholson was one friend who had surpassed her. Winifred Nicholson (a crayon portrait of her by Cooie hung on the stairs) another. As a young girl and 'poor relation' (her father was a clergyman) she had stayed much at Renishaw and Montegufone with the Sitwells, and told endless and loving stories of them; of 'Sashie' hiding under her bed from some night-terror, of some god-like young man over whom she and Edith had together sighed. A poet whom I met in London—Keidrich Rhys it was—and who visited me at Cooie's house had recently been 'taken up' by Edith Sitwell, and Cooie asked him to remember her to the poetess. He must have written to her, for he later showed me the letter he had received in reply; one of the unkindest letters I have ever read, saying, in effect, how extraordinary that the creature should still exist, 'like some old nanny or household retainer', I think the phrase was, whom one had forgotten all about long ago. *Le mieux* could be very cruel to *le bien*. I am bound to say that Ben Nicholson was not—that he visited Cooie, enjoyed her humour, and wasn't wanting in gratitude or loyalty for those kindnesses received before fame which are so usually forgotten after.

Her health—and the air-raids—became worse; and Cooie was at last persuaded to go into a nursing-home in the country. I visited her there and was shocked at the change in her: she had the dying look, and although she was talking with eager hope of returning (in the care of a nurse) to her country cottage near her old home in Berkhamsted, she died on the day following her arrival there. Perhaps she had been kept alive only by the longing she had to return to the place of her childhood: *querencia*. That is how her house in Paulton's Square came to be mine; I took over the lease

174

from her executors, and, by small but painful instalments, bought such of her furniture as her heirs did not want. She left me, too, a small Ben Nicholson painting; I sold it later (for too little) to pay my children's school fees. I had to sell everything I ever had of value, from a drawing Henry Moore gave me from his Shelter notebook, down to my last review-copy; indeed I was always utterly lost when it came to earning money. Since the things I wanted to do were not things for which money is paid, I have sometimes, in moments of desperation, had to compromise. But on the whole I have kept my vow to do nothing for money I would not have done for its own sake. I remember once saying something to George Orwell about those with inner wealth not caring so much about the material kind; thinking, no doubt, of my father's people and their unworldly values; and he replied, 'Yes, but those with material wealth don't have the same need of the inner kind.' At the time I saw in this only a paradox of wit; it did not occur to me then, nor for years after, that there could be human beings above the level of the blindest ignorance who could seriously prefer material to immaterial riches. Much later I was struck by an observation in one of Jung's books, that an extrovert in solitary confinement would become in the end an introvert; and an introvert, surrounded by all the pleasant things of life, an extrovert. I wondered then for a moment what I would have become in other circumstances; but then, I made my circumstances by what I was, and chose, from moment to moment and from day to day; as do all.

Cooie's house came to me with her blessing, and the blessing she had herself inherited from those who came before her. The house had belonged to Mrs. Comyns-Carr, friend of Mrs. Patrick Campbell. Henry James, it was said, had stood before the little Georgian fire-place of what was now to be my room; the house had its story and its life. It was my wish and intention to deserve my spiritual inheritance, and the pear-tree and the vine Cooie had loved. Not only was this my intention in what I there should write, but in the blessing I hoped would come to whoever entered under my roof. For, like Martindale vicarage, this house too seemed to me given, by a miracle, and to those from whom it came I felt myself in duty bound to use what they gave as they would have wished.

Very often I would hear the door-bell ring, usually at night, when there was no one there. I thought nothing of it, not even that it was odd; I used to suppose I had simply been mistaken. It was, all the same, very persistent, as I have realized only since living in another house whose door-bell does not ring except when someone rings it. If it was Cooie Lane who visited her old house on those occasions, I never saw her; but a few years after her death I had a vivid dream of her. In my dream she was in a charming garden-house or arbour; and, as in life, full of humour, and at the same time happy with a kind of serene gaiety; she reproached me, saying 'you have not remembered me for a long time, have you?'—which was true. The flavour, the atmosphere of the dream was indescribably yet unmistakably that of Cooie; but this quality, which convinced me that this was no ordinary dream, I cannot communicate.

Two other dreams of this character I have had. One was of a friend who had died in the belief that there is no survival; 'when we are dead we are finished,' I remember his saying to me, bitterly and passionately, not long before his last illness. In my dream this friend appeared, dreadfully unhappy, convinced of *being dead*: 'I am *dead*,' he said in the dream; and believing himself so was confined within this terrible fantasy.

The third dream too was characterized by the quality of the spirit who, as I supposed, visited me: Edwin Muir. The dream came on Christmas eve, 1960, almost a year after his death. I was a child in a village, wet and wintry; a dream-village woven no doubt from memories of childhood winters at the Manse, and also it may be from the village of Swaffham Prior, where Edwin and Willa Muir were living at the time of his death; and my knowledge that he like myself had been a country child. I had, in my dream, to guide Edwin across intricate footpaths and low wire fences, and other

176

small foot-entangling obstacles; but then he began to lead, and I followed him to a stone building, a *broch*, or fort, or perhaps only an old stone barn; yet ancient, with a quality of anonymous ancestral dignity. Edwin now climbed with ease the stone wall, to enter the upper floor; and with an effort, I followed him. In front of me he went on into a great empty loft, without windows or doors, and in darkness. From the far end of this great hall or loft there blew towards us a warm gentle wind of indescribable fragrance, and I exclaimed, 'It's the breath of the spirit.' Edwin went on before me in the direction from which that sweet wind was blowing, until he came to the far wall which was not, like the others, of stone, but a thin partition. This he merely touched, and it fell away, and then he was no longer there; but beyond lay the fields of spring radiant in the rising sun. I looked into that far-distant sunrise with the knowledge 'there I must also go'; but my time had not come.

At about the same time as I found shelter with Cooie Lane, I also found a niche in another, and more civilized, wartime department, and if I did not, here either, quite grasp what I was expected to do (still less know how to do it) I nevertheless passed unnoticed; perhaps because the head of my department was, this time, a pleasant young man interested in literature, and with some notion of becoming a publisher after the war. Therefore he treated me, as a poet, with a certain respect to which as whatever I was called in his department I certainly had no title. This department was situated in Bush House; but the hierarchies of administration, all those partitions and typing-pools, seemed to me more unreal than any dream. I never believed it to be anything more substantial than a place in some modern allegory—*The Castle*, for example—or rather a non-place, so little did it seem related to the reasons for which human souls enter this world and pass through it; yet down in the canteen in the basement one saw faces (all nullified in the artificial light of that subterranean place) as out of context as my own; Manya Harari, who was later to publish the works of Teilhard de Chardin; Rafael Nadal, who had been Lorca's friend and was, many years later, to become mine. I suppose I must have seen there—though I did not know it—Simone Weil also.

I met there Antonia White; far more experienced in the ways of such non-places than I was, and incomparably more skilled at impersonating the person she was expected to be. She was, I am bound to say, very kind to me; and certainly she, and Graham Greene, who presently also appeared in the Department (for this kind of thing was, as he himself admitted, 'copy' for the books he wrote or might write) influenced the course of my life at that time. If their influence put me off my true course that was my fault, not theirs, for they acted towards me in good faith and with the utmost kindness.

Yet for me that period in Bush House was a betrayal into a most subtle insincerity. Flung into a world where I had to survive not by being what I was but by trying to simulate some other kind of creature than a country child who had grown up into a poet, I panicked; I thought I must play a role, or perish. If the child I was in Northumberland, if the poet of Martindale I may call my real self, that real self, in the years of Bush House, I once again betrayed. Perhaps those years concerned only what Yeats calls the Mask, my outward personality; for when I try to recall them, I do not seem to live or re-live what I remember but rather to see myself as an unreal figure moving among other unreal figures, a shadow among shadows. If any one of those shadowy figures seems real, it is Antonia, not myself.

I had been happy at Martindale because there I had been permitted to be, for that heaven-sent time, simply what I was; and solitude was to me then, and has at all times been, a supreme happiness because only in solitude can I be entirely natural; like some enchanted seal who, alone, can emerge from my seal-skin and bathe in my native element. I have no other milieu in which I can be myself, I am more or less of a stranger (an 'outsider') everywhere. Helen Sutherland it was—and she too had lived much alone— who put into words what few realize about solitude: that it

178

is the most intensely lived of all states. To it belong our deepest thoughts, prayer and poetry are of it; even love; for how seldom, when the real person is present, can we say those things that the heart says to the beloved in solitude?

Hitherto I had supposed myself to be invisible to others; an illusion which had served me well enough; I do not know how well it had served others, for my mantle was not some grey mist of silence, but a curious motley, a patchwork, perhaps the 'cat-skin' of the fairy-tale, made up of scraps taken from the pelts of a multitude of beasts. But now, in London, in order to survive at all, I must simulate some other person, or perish. I had now, so I thought, quickly to make myself into something other than myself, for money-making purposes, since the poet could quite obviously not hope to survive as such; but only by the help of whatever other self I could extemporize. For what, in this world, is weaker than the spirit of poetry? Yet in the end it has been my only strength. I have sometimes wished I had tried less hard to become a beast of burden—been, like David Gascoyne, or like Tambimuttu, unemployable. I was too moral, yet not moral enough; too much a poet, yet not enough a poet; too weak, yet not weak enough to ask, as I should have done, for supernatural help.

Antonia White, sensitive to an extreme degree within and behind it, had a mask which she had, so it seemed to me, cultivated with extreme attention and meticulous care. She seemed to carry it in her hands walking on tip-toe, like a precious piece of glass she was afraid of breaking. She gave thought to how she moved, sat down, got up, crossed a room, like an actress giving careful thought to a part she was learning. All she did was carefully self-conscious to a degree that seemed at times almost perilous, like some delicate feat performed by a juggler. I knew—for David Gascoyne, who was devoted to her, had lent me her *House of Clouds*, and shown me, at the same time, a photograph which caught her off guard—that she was, though a highly trained creature, not a tame one. Behind the mask there was a soul of extreme sensibility.

179

Antonia was a Catholic; and often she talked of the Church. Of her childhood in a convent of the Sacred Heart (Sonia had been educated at the same school some years later), her lapse, and her return, at last, to the Church, she told me. I listened with a mixture of pity and terror, fascination and incredulity. It was—this much at least I recognized —a real story, a real experience of the soul which she so subtly and minutely had undergone. Different as was her destiny from my own, we were, I recognized, alike in having followed the thread of a destiny, in seeing a life as a quest or pilgrimage. I respected her for living her story, but the story itself was strange to me. I felt about it as about Henry James's novels: what were all these invisible bars? Were these cages of the soul not self-constructed, was it not enough to walk, Bagheera-like, out of the cage into freedom? So naïve was I about the human situation; for, much as I knew about the kingdom of nature, I knew next to nothing about the human world. Yet when I used in my own mind the word 'freedom' I did not mean licentiousness and sloth; I meant what Shelley meant, what Blake meant. The soul, so I believed, has its innate form which must unfold according to its own mysterious inner laws; as in nature plant or animal forms. To interfere, by the imposition of external constraints, with this organic unfolding, was the great sin against life; and the only discipline I could recognize was the necessity of attending scrupulously to the voices of intuition, which guide each aright. And yet I was fascinated by Antonia's sincere, subtle, poignantly truthful story of her return to the Church, her voluntary exchange of her freedom for its rule.

Graham Greene too was a Catholic. I had reviewed books for him at the time he was literary editor of the *Spectator*; and now in the Department it was a pleasure to see him tilting against bureaucracy, a game of skill which he played as others play chess, or poker, perhaps. Graham was, towards both Antonia and myself, invariably chivalrous; like a knight who does battle with every champion, but shows courtesy towards women. I cannot say that I at all understood Graham either; he was not of my own imaginative kindred, but the association was, at the time, a very pleasant one.

To this day I do not know what it was that drove me to take the desperate step of becoming a Catholic convert. It was almost like the impulse to jump down from a giddy height, a loss of nerve. My situation I felt to be desperate; something had to be done, for my love had got out of hand. Since we do, by laws however mysterious, attract to ourselves what is appropriate to our inner disposition, Alastair (who never entered my sanctuary of Martindale) did enter the squalor of Percy Street. How this came about I no longer remember; but I well remember that, in hurrying down the dirty blacked-out stairs, unfamiliar and alien, to open the door to his so long-fantasied presence, I blacked my eye on the newel of the banister and greeted him with the painful disfiguring bruise already spreading; say that my daimon was trying to bring me to my senses by a sharp blow; or that unconsciously I gave myself that unheeded salutary warning.

Yet the habit of being in love with him was too strong. The illumination of this delusive passion had brought the world to life; given me those insights from which I had drawn my poetry. I could not relinquish it; I was rather prepared to follow this love to whatever distant goal it might lead, to lay this useless, unrequited—indeed unrequitable—passion upon the altar of sacrifice. Yet could I do this? I wondered; and I thought I could. Only so, I felt, could use be made of this burning love, so useless on earth, so far in excess of the banal biological purposes of the life-cycle. That it was useless absolutely some sense of economy prevented me from imagining; I could not have endured to live, had I thought so. I must offer myself and my otherwise useless passion, to God. But also—if I am truthful—was I not insuring my pride against the possibility, indeed the probability, the all but certainty, of rejection?

It may be that to those who have never overwhelmingly experienced the power of passionate love such an avowal

181

will seem an incomprehensible exaggeration of a straight-forward natural appetite; but those who have will know that I was at that time fighting for my life. Wrong as my course was, I wonder what would have been the right one?

Perhaps, then, as Ulysses had himself tied to the mast as his ship rowed past the sirens (I thought of this comparison at the time) so did I from the Church want only its restraints. I had not in myself the will-power necessary to my own survival; or if I had, needed some outward safeguard of my condition, like a religious habit. Perhaps my hidden motive was defensive, hunted and torn as I was and unable, almost, to live unless I could rid myself of the sexual instinct in one sure and absolute amputation.

But after all, as Antonia so often said, the real question was, did I believe in the truth of Catholic doctrine? She had herself been tormented by innumerable doubts about the truths taught, and had been compelled into faith by her repeated encounters with what seemed sheer miracle. She often amazed me by confessing, for example, her difficulty in believing such stories as that of Genesis, of Adam and Eve and the Tree and the Serpent. Since it would never for a moment have occurred to me to believe in the factual historical truth of this marvellous and inexhaustibly rich mythological narrative, neither would it have occurred to me to doubt it. But, said Antonia, 'we are *supposed* to believe in it as *literal* truth'. This astonished me, as it was so clearly a symbolic allegory, not of the order of historical fact, but of truth of the imagination, expressed figuratively. As a poet this was so self-evident to me that it was impossible for me to become worried about its possible truth or untruth in other senses. Later I went, with Antonia, to a series of lectures on the Apocalypse by a brilliant young Dominican, Father Richard Kehoe; and he defined 'literal truth' as the sense intended by the author of the book, as against personal interpretations. But it was, among my Catholic acquaintance, considered 'brave' to open profound truths where ignorance could at best read a fairy-tale, and at worst, blindly believe nonsense. So it was with the Immaculate

182

Conception, the Virgin Birth, and so on. When the doctrine of the Assumption of the Virgin was propounded I was surprised to discover the number of my acquaintance, Catholic as well as Protestant, to whom this was a stumbling-block. To me it seemed absurd to find one aspect of a total symbolic event less acceptable than other parts; mythical events (so I thought) are not to be verified (did they or did they not take place) but rather to be understood, as is poetry. If anything I still continued to find the Christian myth, as compared with the pagan richness of symbol, too meagre, and welcomed any addition. If physical fact had been in question—if the Virgin Birth were a parthenogenesis in the sense in which biologists use the term of a pheno-menon commonly met with in the reproduction of echino-derms, and occasionally, I seem to remember, recorded of rabbits, why found a religious doctrine upon it? As literal fact such events would have no meaning at all; how deduce the 'divinity' of an incarnation from a biological anomaly? When in antiquity heroes were called the 'sons' of this or that god, the meaning plainly was that they partook of the nature of Apollo or Zeus or Asclepius; and it might indeed be—and so I believed it was—that the nature of the Most High, the Logos, might become incarnate in human form. If a divine order exist at all, such an Incarnation must be possible, once, or many times, as the Indian religions teach; or every time, as Blake believed.

No doubt I misconceived Catholic Christianity altogether, and what I in reality believed was the doctrine of the neo-Platonists, of which, however, I knew at that time very little: I had read Inge on Plotinus, a little of Plato, but not the Enneads, and none of the other Platonic philosophers. But I could say the creed, after my fashion; and how else, after all, should a poet believe in symbols?

All these questions were in fact so many irrelevances; for the real lack of realization in me was of quite a different kind: I had no moral sense, no charity, no 'grace'. Whatever my stupidities may have been, they were not of an intellectual order. On the contrary, my mistake was to imagine that intellectual understanding was all-sufficient, and that nothing more was required. But although I could argue myself into a logical acceptance of Christianity, never could I argue myself into a love for the Christian mythology; even, with sorrow I admit it, for the figure of Jesus as presented by the Church; the dwelling on wounds and mutilations and martyrdoms. So deep was my early distaste for, and fear of, the Christian religion that although my mind could be persuaded, my imagination continued to reject Christianity. Nevertheless, there was no alternative for me, Christianity being the religion of the civilization into which I was fortunate, unfortunate, foolish or wicked enough (all these possibilities are considered both by Plotinus and by the Indian sages) to have been born. Of Catholicism as a culture I may have had some conception; but of Christianity as a way of life, something simple not to be found in books at all—that secret I had not discovered.

Graham Greene too was tormented by 'doubts', though less subtle than Antonia's, for he was a convert, and his mind had been formed, as had mine, on simpler lines than those fine Jesuitical intricacies which James Joyce so nostalgically depicts. I remember his saying to me once (we were walking together through some woods and fields near Berkhamsted and I can remember his voice and his look as he quoted the words, one of my few flashes of imaginative insight into Graham Greene) 'Unless I shall see in His hands the print of the nails, and put my finger into the print of the nails, and thrust my hand into His side, I will not believe.' It was from Graham also that I first heard of Padre Piä, who bore the stigmata. It is obvious that for one of the types of mankind, this proof by physical evidence is crucial; to me, I must confess, it really had no importance whether the Incarnation had, as historical fact, taken place or not.

Graham insisted that Catholicism is essentially a 'magical' religion. I did not quite see what he meant, but had nothing against magic, as such. Transubstantiation, however, did not strike me as a magical, but as a metaphysical doctrine.

Again, I regarded with intellectual scorn (in this case surely justified) a certain Anglican bishop much discussed in my childhood who had offered to disprove the doctrine by a chemical analysis of the consecrated bread. What did he expect to find? I preferred an Irishman's answer (it was Louis MacNeice who told me) to the question 'How can bread be God?'—'What else would it be?'

I think my reasons (such as were not downright bad) strangely insufficient. There may have been others of which I was, and remain, unaware; the wish, for example, to please Helen Sutherland. Had I not myself seen and admired David Jones's immersion in Catholic culture? And Eliot, too, not a Catholic but assuredly a Christian. The need, unconfessed and scarcely recognized, of some kind of human context, suddenly felt in the nightmare-world of London; a desperate fear of sinking. For those whom birth and upbringing has predestined to no other, the *civitas dei* is, I suppose, the only society of which we may become members.

Why then did I not embrace some form of Theosophy, or one of the Indian religions? I very much wish I had done so. But—apart from my doubtless neurotic need for self-immolation, my wish to please Helen Sutherland, and my admiration for Antonia and my other new Catholic friends —I must plead in justification for what I knew at the time, and can now see far more clearly, to have been the wrong course, that I lived, as it were, upon the watershed between the Christian era and what is now called the Age of Aquarius. Christendom had inspired all the great art of the civilization to which I belonged; and, God knows, in adopting Catholic so-to-say nationality I was in one respect sincere—in my total rejection of the materialist philosophies. It was less obvious, then, than now, that the Christian era, with all its greatness, was at an end. Yet, as a poet, it was for me to have divined this; and I did know it. David Jones (whom I see as the last artist of Christendom, though not necessarily the last Christian artist, in England) was on one side of that watershed; his love for the traditions, the culture of

Christendom was sincere. Mine was not. Yet again I failed to be truthful through cowardice.

Gay Taylor disapproved of my rash and ill-judged, histrionic and insincere 'conversion'. She said my character and my temper became much worse when I was being a Catholic. She herself, keeping the thread of her own 'way' always under her sensitive touch, read the Christian mystics, indeed, far more deeply and constantly than I did; but she also kept the *Tao*, the way of effortless wind and water, the 'way of heaven and earth'. She also said that the Catholic Church had shed too much blood to have remained under any divine blessing; the blood of heretics and of Jews. As in Cambridge I had made the mistake of thinking civilization immutable, so now I made the same mistake, thinking that because the truths of Christinaity are eternal, belonging to the nature of things, the Church also must be immutable. Had I attended to the signs how easily I could have seen—indeed I did very clearly see, and yet behaved as though I did not see—that the spirit was moving in other places, not in the old forms any longer.

Gay told me of a 'divine dream' she had had; which, even now, I recall as vividly as if it had been my own. The dreamer —Gay, that is—was struggling across a dark, low tract of country, called in her dream by the Bunyan-like name of 'Broadmarsh'. She toiled on, coming at last to just such a small, low-built but very ancient church as those she loved, in waking life, to visit; for the sake of rustic architecture or (in the vicar's absence) to pray there. She entered the church; where, to her amazement, she found an interior of rich glory of crimson and gold, and a great archangel depicted on the vaulted roof. Overcome with awe she exclaimed, 'It's a *cardinal*'—knowing the word to mean, one of the four archangels who guard the cardinal points or directions of space. The words were then said to her, 'a church in the hearts of men'. This was her 'shewing'; so much deeper, so much truer, than my foolish plunge into the Catholic Church, itself at best only a symbol and a creation of 'the church in the hearts of men'.

Years later, after one of my many periods of vacillation, I went to consult Marco Pallis (himself a Buddhist, but a member of that group who, following Réné Guénon and Frithjof Schuon, disseminate the high doctrine of the transcendent unity of all the 'revealed' religions). Marco assured me that, distasteful as Christianity might be, none of the other traditions were in better shape: in the last age of the Kali-yuga, all were in a state of decadence. Yet all (and this God knows I have never doubted) do teach the perennial truth; differently envisaged, each in a manner appropriate to one or another civilization. Born a European, logic (and the Hindu view of rebirth for that matter, no birth being accidental or out of place) demanded that, unless for some quite exceptional reason, I should be a Christian. Reluctantly I accepted Marco's verdict and went, half-hearted still, once again back to the Church; whose teachings, so far as that goes, I have never doubted. I have believed too much, not too little, for Catholic orthodoxy. But no freedom less than absolute is freedom at all: the poet has no right—no soul has the right—to surrender free-will.

An Indian friend and Vedantist, Dr. Arabinda Basu, from whom I learned something of Indian thought (an atmo-sphere in which I have always been able to breathe, whereas trying to be a Christian is, for me, like trying to live under water) said to me, just before his return to India and the *ashram* of his guru Sri Aurobindo, 'Don't let the Church get you back.' But I did; over and over again I have failed at that test of courage and honesty. Even now it is almost more than I can do to admit to myself—as in honesty to those who may read these words I must admit—that, finally, I have found myself unable to remain in the Church.

I am, of course, looking years ahead. Certainly my true place is with the esoteric tradition of neo-Platonism, Cab-bala, Theosophy. There my heart, which so sinks in the presence of Christian works of devotion, of most Christian art, and, alas, most practising Christians, leaps in joyful recognition. No. Every civilization, not excepting European

187

Christendom, comes to its term. Only the eternal is ever living, not any one of its expressions in time.

To write this costs me much; not to have written so would have cost me my integrity; already too often compromised in this matter. For an unbeliever not to be a Christian is a simple matter, and agnostics and atheists may well wonder why I have taken so long to make so easy a rejection; but for the believer—and God knows I have never for a moment wavered in my belief in a spiritual order—it is not a simple or an easy thing to say, 'I cannot make a Christian of myself'. Perhaps all I am revealing is that for all my super-subtleties, I have been loveless and never found that simple secret known to all loving hearts.

Yet another need may have in part determined my course: the need in my desperate state to talk to some wise person, some spiritual adviser and counsellor. The time was past when I would have sought help from any Freudian; and even had I known any Jungian at that time—which I did not—I would not have accepted any view of suffering or sin which seeks to reduce these aspects of life to terms not of personal responsibility but of 'mental illness'. No, I preferred and I still prefer, the heroic Christian morality which sees in these the stuff of life; in sin, failures for which we are responsible; in suffering, a task, a bearing of the world's burden and a transmutation of its base matter into spiritual gold; a privilege whose purposes are beyond our knowledge which we yet intuitively divine to be of supreme importance in the total spiritual economy of the world. I did not want to rid myself of suffering but to learn how to use it; for above all things I could not bear to suffer in vain. It still seems to me the chief glory of Christianity that it sees in suffering a positive value. Buddhism offers release from suffering; Christianity the Cross, heavy with all the anguish of the world, to be lived and known as the very heart of a Mystery. I wished to understand that mystery, not to be freed from it.

I was told (by Manya Harari, in the canteen of Bush House, it was) that Father Pius Dolin, prior of the Carmelites in Kensington, was a priest of great holiness; and to the obscure door opening onto the pavement of Church Street, symbol of all doors of sanctuary, I went, and was admitted. I remember him as for the first time he entered the little bare parlour where I was received by him for instruction. Father Pius is one of the most beautiful, most spiritually transfigured beings I have ever met. He had a way of entering the parlour with a kind of grace of gesture, like a saint in some Italian painting, yet without himself, so I would suppose, being in the least aware of it; rather as if the painters of those figures had caught the gestures and bodily postures natural to certain states of the human soul; the stillness of those who are, as it were, listening, attending inwardly; a suave grace expressive of calm of mind and charity, the control of a moment by moment dedication and submission of the self to the Self. Those who daily celebrate Mass must come to be aware of the body itself as a kind of living icon, whose gestures are expressive, not only in a general but in a specific way, like the *mudras* of Hindu sculptures and dance; gestures not natural to the once-born, but natural to the twice-born; at the same time beautiful and impersonal, expressive and formal. The natural man has been taken over by the spiritual, the I by the not-I. In Father Pius I for the first time divined—though only dimly, and without realizing the immense significance of what I saw—that the conformity of the natural man, at every moment of a life-time, to a religious rule, far from destroying a personality, truly creates one; whereas the spontaneity of 'self-expression', the 'natural' behaviour of the undisciplined, does exactly the reverse; as the apparent 'naturalness' of a dancer is the supreme triumph of art over nature. What a barbarian I still was! For with Father Pius there before my eyes to prove that 'he that loseth his life the same shall find it', I still clung to my notions of freedom, the 'freedom' of the soul to grow in its own way, by its own innate laws. Nor did I yet realize what I have since slowly and painfully been forced to recognize, that the spiritual Way is, like every art, against nature, not with it, up-stream against the current, the hard way. But I still had a truly Protestant horror of conforming to an external rule; the self-imposed rule of the dedicated poet, I said to myself, is higher and better than the merely external discipline these Carmelites assume. And so perhaps it is, but, in the long run it, too, no less austere, leads 'out of nature'.

Father Pius was Irish, with a round and (in its physical features) almost comical face; yet he seemed to be overflowing with the energy of an inward joy, irrespressible; he was habitually at once grave and joyful; and in him I recognized some quality above human intelligence, and far above human knowledge. What he knew, so it seemed to me, was not his own mind, but the 'other' mind, the other Self, which poets know as the imagination, but Christian visionaries call Christ. 'Jesus the Imagination,' Blake writes, boldly equating the two names. Once he told me that the gift God had given him was 'the discernment of spirits', insight into souls.

Just as his understanding seemed to come from another level of mind than his own, so did the continuous sense of joy which his presence communicated, as from some source beyond himself to which he was transparent just insofar as he submitted entirely his human personality to its irradiation. This was a kind of love higher, as I recognized, than earthly eros; and yet, not to have looked down those long vistas of the wonders of creation seemed to me then a pure loss which I could not, for myself, have contemplated. Those other vistas which the saints describe in vain to those who have not themselves seen them, I could not measure. Thus I was in two minds, even in the presence of the freedom and *caritas* of sanctity.

So Father Pius instructed me in the catechism; and how gentle he was with my bruised soul, how charitable, never blaming me, nor condemning the earthly passion which had swept me to the door of the Carmelites. And, talking with this son of perhaps some Irish cabin, how at home I felt, not only with the language of the spirit which he spoke but, no less, with that world from which he had come,

190

the world of country people where, somewhere behind the ascetic life of the monastery, was the sense of home, of the family, brothers and sisters and father and mother, the human pattern somehow, somewhere, right. And how, even though my own life, but for a few years of my childhood, had never run true, I seemed to remember it all, with a nostalgia all the greater for the broken pattern which in imagination I was all the time trying to restore, but which in actuality I never was able to restore. There was something behind the Carmelite monk which belonged to Bavington, and the Manse kitchen where old copies of *The Northern Presbyter* were kept under the cushion of the rocking-chair; to fetching the milk in the evening, and water from the stone village well in buckets kept in the back kitchen; an earthly restoration of all things to their proper places. How express that sense one has, in the presence of sanctity, of a remembered familiarity, of this being just as it all should have been?

Marco Pallis has somewhere written that the sacramental quality of anything whatsoever is the norm from which creation has fallen with the Fall of man; the change from the sacramental to the profane way of experiencing the whole of the created world being the Fall itself; a narrowing of consciousness, a forgetting. In this sense the holy bread and wine of the Christian Mass are what bread and wine essentially are, unperceived by us. In Father Pius saintliness seemed a return to the lost norm, to things as they truly are. He had a kind of simplicity, remote indeed from the insolent familiarity of the profane world, where the assumption is that our neighbour is as vile as ourselves. On the contrary, he made me feel that nothing can be simpler than to meet all on the ground of the Holy Spirit, the only ground of every being, and therefore more familiar, more native than the world, so strangely alien, in which I lived my outer life. A story I remember his telling me—to illustrate what point I do not know—has strangely impressed itself, for all its simplicity, upon my memory. It communicated to me, in his telling of it, some quality that may elude my re-telling;

191

something which the modern profane world has all but lost. The story was of a nine- or ten-year-old Irish girl whose father was a poor man who sold vegetables from a cart. One day as she was coming to find him, in the market, there was some trouble, and she had to see the police (was it? or other ruffians) beating and striking 'the poor old man, her father. And at that moment, she grew up.' That was all the story; it is the same, with countless variations, that is told and re-told in Christian art, of the brutality of the profane world to the human soul, ever defenceless. But what perhaps makes me remember the story when I have forgotten so much else is the fullness of the relationship it implied, in one of the most simple and fundamental of all, that of father and daughter; and the breath it brought from an almost lost world in which a family is a community of human souls, loving one another. The relationship so described was natural, indeed archetypal, but realized to the full in that uncomplicated simplicity in which alone depth of feeling can exist. My own family relationships, complicated and embittered—the uprooting had begun a generation before I was born, many generations perhaps—precluded that simplicity and depth. My own relationship with my father should have been like that, but was not; yet it was not—was it?—only or all my fault that it had been so impaired. When and where had I lost the thread of those simple relation-ships of love, husband and wife, father and mother and children, brothers and sisters? Of Adam's household, whose natural affections and bonds the Catholic religion has protected through time, in all those countries where its culture has nourished the lives of the people? For—such is the paradox—only in a supernatural context does the natural thrive. True, the story might have been told (but for its ending—the girl became a nun, the obviously most practical thing she could do being to assist by her prayers the souls of mankind, whose bodies must suffer such indignities) of my father's Methodist people, though hardly of the Church of England where the absolute dignity of man is obscured by class-distinction of a rather petty and provincial kind, unknown within the greater Church, accustomed to treating kings and emperors no otherwise than other sons of Adam. Yet, within the Catholic context, it seemed to me to stand out clear of any reformist political sentimentality. No political or social moral was to be drawn; only the naked truth of the human condition, within the context of a religion that protects and saves souls from the world, though it cannot save bodies from the conditions of the world. What the girl had seen in the moment in which, as Father Pius said, she had 'grown up' was the basic truth also of the Buddhist religion, a truth irremovably grounded in the nature of the temporal world, 'Life is suffering'; and with that insight, compassion. Those only who have understood and accepted this truth, and fully felt the violation that cruelty is to those beings who in love's eyes are of infinite value, can be said to have 'grown up'. Many see the suffering without the value, out of context. A strayed Irish bard, from the same world, who about the King's Road was cleaning cars for the price of a drink, asked what he thought of the contemporary English 'angry' social drama replied in a phrase whose roots are in that ancient traditional wisdom, 'Better than anger an elegant sorrow that suffers all.'

But I could only look from afar at the integrity of Adam's family. Had I myself lived by the ancient pattern I would never have come to the door of the Carmelites at all; for to become a Catholic only isolated me still further from the natural bonds and simple relationships of home, and widened every gulf in my life, while at the same time giving me no context, natural or intellectual (since my mind had been formed in other patterns) in which I could live my life more simply. Catholicism was, for me, but one more complication, one more break in the pattern.

On the night before I was to be received into the Church—upon the Feast of the Epiphany—my daimon visited me. I was, so he told me, doing wrong, going against everything he and those greater ones who had at times visited me, had wished for me, demanded of me, given me. I was about to separate myself from the inspirers, from those free spirits of

193

imagination, those intellections who shun prison-bars, and all man-made restrictions and conditions imposed upon the reality which they mediate and express. All this and more my daimon said to me; and can you, he asked, can you really form and fashion your imagination by those symbols to which you are about to bind yourself? And will you part from us, from the elementals who companioned your childhood, from the celestial hierarchies whose natures are free, as you were free in your childhood, and as you are— yes—as the poet in you is free even now? Do you really love those tame saints, so monotonously good, so wingless? Do you not, then, understand what a precious gift is the freedom of the imagination, indeed more than a gift, a sacred trust, given only to chosen ones, and, among these, to the poets? You know—so my daimon continued—that the difference between yourself and your new Catholic friends (not our friends, however, the daimon said) lies precisely in this, that you are one who has been given the freedom of the poet to attend, directly, to our voices. You are betraying us, and you yourself we will leave, we will be compelled to leave you, down there in the world you have chosen. Your humility, not your pride, is false, a cowardly evasion; to rise to what is demanded of you calls for a greater humility, for it demands that you entrust yourself to us; do you suppose that you can do anything, great or small, without our inspiration? In humbling yourself you are an egoist, safe- guarding yourself, through imaginative sloth and moral cowardice, behind a barrier of foregone conclusions, from the holy spirit. When will human beings know that great things are demanded of them, not face-saving conformity?

I knew this was the voice of truth. Not a word did the daimon say about sex or Alastair, one way or the other; it was not upon the issue of passionate love that they tempted, or admonished me; their words came from a place beyond all that, and this I knew, and mourned with them that last night; the friends and companions of that freedom I was about to forgo, as I then feared, for ever.

And what did I answer? 'Yes, I know,' I said, 'everything
194

you tell me is true. But now I am committed, now I have promised, now it is all arranged.' I had experienced the disastrous consequences of two mistaken marriages, and yet I was prepared, for a third time, to try to deceive the daimon, to go, deliberately and wilfully, against the warning of conscience. 'How,' I continued, 'can I fail Father Pius, that saintly man—even you must admit that.' ('Yes,' said my daimon, 'but that is not *your* way.') What else I said I do not know; I think I raised the subject of Alastair, in a rather overstrained stage-voice telling them of the renunciation I was about to make of my great love; but they were not listening; and so, all night, I lay awake in the little back bedroom in Paulton's Square, with the pear-tree outside my window in the night, dark and leafless. We mourned together, the inspiring spirits of life and I; I knew they were about to leave me, and could only bid them farewell. But I tempted Providence when I said to them, 'but we will meet again—not now, but someday.'

I went through with it, of course; in a kind of daze; I can scarcely remember the occasion, even though it was Father Pius who received me; Antonia, Graham Greene and Robert Speaight afterwards took me out to lunch; Antonia gave me a mantilla, and Robert Speaight *The Ascent of Mount Carmel*. I was stunned by the strangeness of it all.

For years after I would dream, from time to time, that I was in a prison, sentenced (often for murder) for a term of years, and wake in terror, relieved to find that, in the outer world at all events, this was not so. Sometimes the same nightmare horror would be that, in the dream, I found myself to be married; for marriage was, to me, a symbol of imprisonment. I knew in my heart that freedom is a state, a blessing, a task which I had yet again relinquished, sacrificed.

But Father Pius—that was quite another matter. I recollect that bare parlour, and the Carmelite church itself, as a place permeated by the presence of the spiritual world, a place where prayer had called down that Presence. During an air-raid the Church was destroyed by a bomb; I rushed there, in my lunch-hour, this time to offer what comfort my presence could bring to my comforter. There he stood, in his brown habit, among the ruins; where a few others had come, as I had myself. He looked at me, and smiled gravely; grieved, but not at all perturbed to see his church in ruins.

I discovered when I attempted to use the symbolic structure provided by the Church that I was, quite simply, unable to project into these outer forms my own inner life. For me it was all a make-believe in which I could not make myself believe; I could not wed the reality of my inner life to the forms; in attempting to use verbal forms of prayer I became unable to pray at all. I know that the great symbols of Christendom still live for many. An English friend, not even a Protestant, not a believer at all, told me how, on a visit to Prague, she had seen, in one of the churches there, an old woman praying. Her eyes were fixed in loving adoration upon some baroque Christ; and my friend saw the lips of the statue move in answer. Another friend—again not a Catholic, though a believer—was given a medal of the Blessed Virgin which had been blessed by a very holy Spanish nun. She was herself at the time in a condition of intense concentration upon a spiritual and emotional problem of her own; and, sitting with the medal and looking at it, she saw, to her astonishment, brownish-red drops running down from the extended hands of the Virgin onto her own fingers which held it. She wiped the drops from her fingers and found that they were blood; and together with this physical manifestation, she seemed to understand some profound mystery of love and suffering. To her the symbol had spoken, the outward form was at one with some interior reality; but for me this has never been so, my relationship with the archetypal world has been something quite apart from the forms of Catholic iconography. Neither have the forms brought me to the archetypes, nor the archetypes to the symbolic forms of the Christian religion. For me they have held no magic—which is to say, have not been animated from within. What this proves I do not know, but truth compels me to record it. I have come

196

more and more to realize that I have to meet these arche-typal forms in their interior world, where they are free and mysterious; not in those images, plastic or merely con-ceptual, in which they are reflected outwardly, be these portraits as life-like as may be. I respect those whose inner life is happily married to some outer pattern; but at the same time, I also accept, finally, with a certain joy, my own im-posed conditions, which are different from theirs.

Catholic Christendom, like an ancient vine-stock, may be the enduring root of Western European civilization; and yet a true sense of tradition (in terms of living reality not of merely abstract argument) must include the knowledge of where we ourselves are situated within it, and that is not a matter so much of choice as of fact. An attempt to re-graft ourselves can only produce preciosity of taste, antiquarian-ism, or the false note struck by Belloc, Chesterton or Evelyn Waugh, conscientious objectors to their own cultural inheritance. Shakespeare and Milton, not Dante, were my ancestors, Shelley and Coleridge my next-of-kin. Yeats was closer to me than Catholic Joyce; for in Yeats, as in the English romantic poets, the poetry is winged towards 'knowledge absolute'; and his great bell-beat stirred in me when I came to read his poetry. As a Catholic convert the first thing I did was to buy Yeats's collected poems, like a sick dog looking for grass.

Truth to say—and to write this confession costs me a great deal—I have never felt complete kinship of spirit with any Christian; though with Indian friends, and with a few others, Platonists like myself, or Buddhists, like Marco Pallis, all that I could never explain to any Christian is taken for granted without any explanation at all. Perhaps my Christian friends find a corresponding lack in me; but in the nature of things I cannot know what it is that they might say to one another 'Kathleen has never understood'.

One day I was in the Farm Street Jesuit church—our Department had moved into the neighbourhood of Gros-venor Square, and, coming or going, I often went into that church for a while. On one such occasion I was simply walking through, when, abruptly, my consciousness underwent a curious shift, so that I seemed, while at the same time remaining myself, to be a young nun; younger than I was myself at the time, and standing, so it seemed, in a pleasant sunny garden or orchard of blossoming fruit-trees; in France, as it seemed to me. The nun was wearing a black habit with a white head-dress, somewhat stiff and projecting; Antonia thought I had described the dress of the Dominican nuns, but I am not convinced that this was so, my nun's dress seemed rather different. It was odd how vividly clear the feeling of the shaped head-dress was to me, though I could not see it. The young nun was radiantly happy, with a lightness of heart and uplifting joy. At the same time I was able to compare from within—to measure, as it were—my own being with hers, and I knew myself, for all my experience of sorrow and evil, to know much more, to possess a much greater reach and scope of experience than she; though I had lost that bird-like innocent joy which she, in her smaller sphere, had been able to attain or retain. I do not tell this experience as 'evidence' for reincarnation—it might be taken so, but there could be many other possible explanations; insight, for example, of a telepathic kind into another soul, of the present or of the past, to whom I was for the moment attuned, in some respect. Or it could have been simply a symbolic configuration, a kind of waking dream. I tell it not for its curiosity but for its content as an experience; for it expressed the plain truth of my real situation: I was trying to evade, to hide myself in the clothing of a novice, from my true destiny. We cannot, alas, reverse the direction of growth, try to make ourselves smaller than we are out of some false sense of humility, or from cowardice. That young nun's experience of pure joy was not, now, or ever again, for me: not that joy, that walled garden and those flowering apple-trees under the sun of France.

Thirty or more years later I unexpectedly 'remembered' (whether the memory was my own or another's I cannot say, the experience was in either case the same) the same nun's life. Now she was an old woman, who needed the support of a stick to walk across her cell; which, on this occasion, I saw as clearly as I can remember the bedroom I slept in as a child. I could 'see' on one side, her bed, covered with a white counterpane of rough texture; opposite, a prayer-desk, and above this a crucifix with a heavy crown of thorns; a shelf with a few devotional books; on another wall a picture of the Madonna and the child Jesus, whose halo contained the form of the equal-armed cross. High up were windows, and the lovely light in the sky suggested, again, France. There were swifts or swallows crossing that high glimpse of sky. A door opened into, I think, the cloisters. And there she had lived her life, and kept her faith. She was not a rebel; only, ever so little, bored. She had a devotion to the Child Jesus; and as she crossed her cell, supported by her stick, I knew that her other hand held, in imagination, the hand of the *Puer Eternus*. I do not think she would have wished to be a nun again; am I, is my life, what she wished? If so, I hope she felt—as I feel—that, with all its appalling mistakes my life has been richer than those long sinless cloistered days.

CHAPTER NINE

The End of a Golden String

THE YEARS that followed had no radiance in them; but
the war was over, and 9 Paulton's Square, with Anna's
room, and James's room began to seem like a home.
I set to work to earn money in ways that I hoped would
allow me to call my soul my own—a freedom purchased at
the price of poverty, continual anxiety, and hard ill-paid
work; translation, book-reviewing, evening classes at Morley
College, all the usual improvisations. I was not very good at
any of these things, and laboured at them all *contre coeur*, like
a slave saving up to buy his freedom, but seeming as far
from that end as ever. For a short time I had a job in the
Publications Department of the British Council but the
occupation seemed to me rather less to the point than
translations and book-reviews, which were at all events
honest toil; so I gave it up. That, at all events, was the form
my pride took. I could no more fit myself into the world on
its own terms than into the Church. So I remained, poor
and proud, as it seemed to myself; to my friends I must have
seemed merely poor and incompetent. Nor had I any great
cause for pride, for my second volume of poems was much
inferior to my first, cut off as I was from my roots, and re-
planted in the alien soil of London and the Church. But to
me it was obvious that the poems I had at that time written
were only a beginning, tentative exercises to keep my hand
in; I felt myself to be the poet of my future poems, and
under a strong sense of teleological obligation. So a plant in
its phase of growth might be said to 'know' that future
flower and seed is its purpose, and this irrespective of

200

whether or not the plant ever comes to flower or the poet to realize a potential maturity. And yet I took great risks in continually deferring the work I intended to do, in order merely to keep myself and my children alive. It might be said that this was inevitable; but I do not think so; there is always time if the state of mind is right, and mine was not right; I was incapacitated by a multitude of unhealed wounds, hopes, and despairs. Heaven knows I was not a rebel; I no more embattled myself in unimportant issues than I sold myself; my instinct, after my failure to find a context in the Catholic religion, was to conserve my deepest thoughts in silence, and disguise myself once again in my cat-skin mantle, my *trompe-l'oeil* persona. Yet I felt it all as a battle to defend something of infinite value from the world in which I struggled to survive. Better to struggle than to sell what was above price; to better the woman at the expense of the poet was something I could not have brought myself to do. Gay Taylor was fond of exclaiming that she 'did not know what she had done in a former life' to incur her present troubles; I had no need to look to former lives to see the operation, in my own, of cause and effect: my situation, my troubles, were self-caused.

My house helped me; it was like a friend, its simple and dignified proportions (barely and shabbily furnished as it was) its vine and its pear-tree silently speaking to me of order and dignity and simplicity and by doing so, imposing them. I had planted near the back door some ferns from Martindale; I had inherited from Cooie Lane the blessing of the house with the vine and the pear-tree she had loved, and for long I continued to live in it as under her roof and protection. And Helen Sutherland, and the Robertses (near neighbours again, Michael now Principal of the teachers' training college of St. Mark and St. John, at the World's End) never let me go. I lived on as if provisionally; something, I believed, must change this long waiting, there must be an end of it. Even now I thought of myself as still a native of Northumberland, of Martindale, of that faraway land where I had not lived as an exile and a stranger. My comfort was the little back garden of my house, its vine, its pear-tree, its jasmin and lily-of-the-valley, its fern from Martin-dale. The brick wall at the end had been that of Sir Thomas More's garden, so it was said; but the sense of holy ground had little to do with the saint; the tree and the vine and the fern spoke to me not of the English Catholic martyrs, but in the older language of my own lost world of nature. It was the earth itself that was holy. Only alone in my few square yards of London garden could I still, in some measure, become a semblance of myself.

At that time I still thought of my exile not as radical, something which belonged to my nature, or to the human situation as such; still I hoped to find again in this world the here and now of being in my right place that I had known at the Manse; and again, even more briefly and precariously, at Martindale. Because I knew I belonged elsewhere, the present was endurable; for I believed my exile would end, that I would, at last, come to my own. Those who in child-hood have known the state of Paradise perhaps always expect to find again what was once so simply there. I recognized the same quality in the poetry of Edwin Muir (and in Edwin himself when later I met him) and, curiously enough—for it takes one child of Paradise to recognize another—appearances notwithstanding, in Herbert Read. In the Herbert Read of the avant-garde I recognized a disguise (albeit a far more convincing one) like my own; Herbert, Edwin Muir and I, none of us had, at heart, ever left our native place.

I remember, too, with deep gratitude how, when I was waiting at 9 Paulton's Square, for Alastair, now returned from the war, and about to visit me, Gay Taylor came to take leave of me, as it almost seemed to both of us. Gay, for many, many years, my fellow-pilgrim, herself by now knew that her journey was towards the Celestial City. At the door she turned to leave me; and said to me, not reproachfully, but lovingly, 'Well, dear Kathleen, good-bye.' And in those words I knew the angels were themselves again taking leave of me. I knew then with absolute clarity that I must not, on any account, marry any Alastair. For once I heeded the message from the Castle.

A friend, having read thus far my story, understandably dissatisfied with so inconclusive a quest, suggested to me that here I ought to pause, to assess my life hitherto. 'So here I was', he would have me say, 'in the middle of my way, in the world of post-war London, having learned . . .' what? But my record is of rejections; of escapes, as it seemed to me; others might say of disloyalties; abandonments, at all events, of all those refuges, intellectual, moral or domestic, within which, from my student years until now, I had attempted to live. Only in that realm of nature that had been mine in my Northumberland childhood, briefly recaptured at Martindale, did I feel in my true place. My wanderings in those other 'states the soul falls into when it leaves Paradise following the serpent' had not given me, in terms of understanding or symbol, the knowledge I had sought through which I might interpret my proper landscape of the soul. One thing at least I had learned in the bitter world of Experience—that everything that befalls us has its cause within ourselves, and is, therefore, and in that sense, be the experience one of joy or of misery, what is our due. If I was impenitent—I had not yet seen myself in the light of the injury I had done to others—neither did I complain, And I had been given, after all, in that world, so much of value, if I could only discover how to use it: the abrasive mental discipline of Cambridge; Mass-Observation's dark visions of the collective mind; Helen Sutherland's aristocratic insistence on 'the best'; and the sanctuary of the Catholic Church, even though that too proved only the brief refuge of Cain the wanderer whose road runs on.

Presently, by another of those seeming miracles by which a change of inner disposition is followed by a corresponding change in the outward course of events, my course became calmer. Blake now became my Virgil and my guide; I took the end of his golden string, and began, with an exhilarating sense of return to duty, to wind it into a ball. Others before and since have found that string longer than they had supposed. As I entered the British Museum each morning, to begin my day's work where Yeats had worked on Blake before me, my heart would give a little leap of pleasure, a sign surely that the work I was doing was the work I was then meant to be doing. I persisted in the winding in of the golden string a great deal more whole-heartedly than I had ever practised the Catholic religion; and felt myself now once again engaged in a serious imaginative task, and no longer play-acting.

Quite early on in my Blake studies Philip Sherrard (who had read a first draft of some of my Blake work, in which I attempted, if I remember rightly, a Jungian interpretation) had lent me the works of Réné Guénon. These had profoundly changed my outlook; for in Guénon I first found clearly defined that 'knowledge absolute' of which every metaphysical tradition is an expression. From Guénon I went on to discover, with still greater delight, the works of Tambi's uncle; I discovered in Coomaraswamy's writings a view of the arts as the proper language of 'knowledge absolute', a knowledge from which they cannot long be separated and live. I now sought for wisdom not in Academe but 'in Watkins's bookshop', where the legendary Michael Robartes knew he would find Yeats whenever he wished to summon him. Mr. Watkins became my friend; lent me copies of some of his own valuable collection of the works of Thomas Taylor the Platonist. His theosophical bookshop in Cecil Court—that University Library of lost knowledge— became for me, as for others before and since, a shrine of wisdom.

Little by little, I found how great is that literature of exact spiritual knowledge, unheeded by literary critics and literary historians alike; and gradually it became clear to me that not only did Blake possess this knowledge and speak that royal language, but that this learning of the imagination is the mainstream from which poets and artists from Orpheus to W. B. Yeats have drawn life. Proust (in a very different context) uses the image of the way in which letters fall into place as words, words into a sentence, when a clue formerly missing is in our hands which reveals relationships and connections of a kind hitherto unsuspected. The learning of the imagination, I now discovered, is of this kind: it rests upon relationships indiscernible to scholarship as such; which can discover only what it already knows may be there.

With amazement and joy I followed the windings of that mainstream of tradition and some of its tributaries; working upstream, as Yeats had done before me, in the British Museum, where now I spent my days. In the North Library where I had at that time a desk piled high with strange books, I felt the golden string forming under my writing fingers as they copied wisdom. The clues, once noticed, were everywhere. Through the General Catalogue I tracked Blake's footprints; Hermes Trismegistus, the writings and translations of Taylor the English Pagan, the *Proceedings* of the Calcutta Society of Bengal, Paracelsus and Fludd and Agrippa, Ovid's *Metamorphoses*; Swedenborg, Dante. But if Cabbalism and Alchemy may be called esoteric I was above all surprised to discover how much ot this tradition lies plain to view, in the writings of Plato, Proclus, Plotinus, Berkeley's *Siris*; and in the works of the poets themselves. Everywhere evident and accessible this knowledge has at all times been for those who have known how to discern it; hidden it must always remain from those who do not.

When long after I visited Mrs. Yeats in Dublin, she confirmed my view of Blake as a supreme teacher within age-old tradition as that to which Yeats had also come. Works of Thomas Taylor (from whom Blake had learned the doctrine of the Neoplatonists) were still on Yeats's book-shelves; it was she herself who had first possessed them. What a marriage-dowry to bring a poet! When I left, Mrs. Yeats wanted to make me some gift; she hovered over a pile of recent books, reprints of Yeats's works, books on Yeats. She said she could not imagine what most of Yeats's 'critics' were talking about, however, and we left the book-pile. No, I said, not a book. I asked her, instead to give me, from her garden where many rare and beautiful spring flowers were in bloom, an *anemone pulsatilla*; the flower at which Thel, in Blake's title-page, looks so thoughtfully as she considers mutability. This flower is an emblem of Adonis, whose myth is woven into Blake's poem with strands from Ovid, Spenser, and Milton, from Agrippa and Plotinus and the alchemists. It seemed to me fitting that so neo-Platonic a flower should be growing in Mrs. Yeats's garden; so she gave me the flower, and I pressed it carefully. It is now preserved in the pages of my own copy of *The Book of Thel*. With it is a fern-like leaf of the *anemone pulsatilla* which grew on Helen Sutherland's terrace, where so often I have walked and thought, and weeded as well. It was not in a library that the flash of recognition came, but on that terrace where, admiring the curving droop of the leaves, I suddenly recognized them as the same as the leaves on the title-page of *Thel*. Blake too must have loved the real flower, and not the mere emblem.

After Mrs. Yeats's death Anne Yeats gave me the book which her mother had, after all, left me: Yeats's copy of Denis Saurat's work on Blake, with marginalia in Yeats's hand. Yet I had met Mrs. Yeats only twice; when, emboldened by a research student who had assured me of her willingness to meet me (without which assurance I would never have intruded myself upon her) I had visited the poet's wife and medium, whose hand had written, at the spirits' bidding, *A Vision*. She had left me alone, for a time, with Yeats's Blake books; then she had come in, bringing with her, as I remember, in one hand a Cona coffee-machine, in the other a hot-water-bottle. The coffee she placed between us, the hot-water-bottle at her back. She had come to talk to me. 'How long is it', she began, 'since you stopped writing poetry?' I said I had not written for some long time, protesting unhappiness in my private life, or something of the kind. 'A poet has no right not to write,' she said; 'You need a rabbit-bolter.' She explained what she meant—you send a ferret or a terrier down the rabbit-hole to make the rabbit come out. 'I was W.B.Y.'s rabbit-bolter,' she said. It was then she told me that 'Tom' (T. S. Eliot) had first told 'W.B.Y.' (so she called him) to read my poems. So after many years—

when I no longer thought of such things—I received Eliot's posthumous acceptance, with Yeats's also.

We talked of Blake; of Thomas Taylor the Platonist. Had I known more, at that time, of those esoteric studies of the Society of the Golden Dawn from which the poet and his wife had drawn their wisdom, how much more I would have asked her! But when, some years later, I had the knowledge, I did not venture to visit her again, hesitating to intrude when I had no longer the pretext of Blake. How wrong I was in this I discovered only too late, by her legacy to me. But to me the greater legacy was that intangible transmission of the sacred trust of the poet. (Later I returned the book to Anne Yeats for the Yeats library; where, I felt, it ought to be.) After all my détours I am always brought back to my own task. All my attempts to exchange poetry for religion or to sacrifice it on the altar of human passion have proved in the end to be grandiose evasion.